Silhouette of Naomi Wood
by Genevieve Ross
East Gloucester, Mass.
August 20, 1915

Robert H. Wilson

The Story Of The Naomi Wood Collection and Woodford Mansion
in Philadelphia's Fairmount Park

JUNE AVERY SNYDER
Volunteer Administrative Director
and
MARTIN P. SNYDER
Trustee

of THE NAOMI WOOD COLLECTION

HAVERFORD HOUSE
Wayne, Pennsylvania

Copyright © 1981 by June Avery Snyder and Martin P. Snyder.

All rights reserved. This book is protected by copyright. No part of it may be reproduced in any manner or by any means without written permission of the authors.

Library of Congress Catalog Card Number 81-83942

ISBN 0-910702-06-3

PRINTED IN THE UNITED STATES OF AMERICA

Acknowledgements

In our researches for this book, Whitfield J. Bell, Jr., Executive Officer of the American Philosophical Society, has been most generous in making available unpublished materials respecting William Coleman, the first owner of Woodford, and Robert Barclay, the son of its second owner; and in joining us in the pages of *Antiques Magazine* in our unsuccessful search for a portrait of Coleman. Edwin Wolf 2nd, Librarian of the Library Company of Philadelphia, John Platt, Librarian of the Historical Society of Pennsylvania, and Peter Parker, Chief of its Manuscript Division, and their staffs, have also been of continuing help over a period of years. The reports of Charles E. Peterson, restoration architect, have illuminated several points. Ward Childs of the Philadelphia City Archives has assisted wherever possible, as have John McIlhenny, Historian of Fairmount Park, and Cissy Scheerer of his department.

Merle Chamberlain, Archivist of the Philadelphia Museum of Art, brought out for review the several files of Fiske Kimball, its Director, and of the Museum itself. Carol Wojtowics, Curator/Archivist of the Philadelphia Contributionship, unearthed material from its minutes and other records. Raymond V. Shepherd, Jr., Administrator, and Hope Henderson, Assistant Administrator of Cliveden, have provided information concerning certain volumes of the former library of David Franks. Gertrude Thomas kindly supplied Barclay information to us, as did F. Otto Haas, the owner of Alexander Barclay's town house. Mildred Fisher's unpublished material on the Fitzwater family, that of William Coleman's wife, was willingly shared with us. Professor Leo Hershkowitz, of Queen's College, New York, offered a number of leads. Webster Evans, because of his interest in George Clymer, joined in the Coleman portrait search; Thomas R. Butler led us to the tenancy of David Hayfield Coyningham.

Mrs. William H. Reeves, daughter-in-law of General Russell Thayer, former Chief Engineer and Superintendent of Fairmount Park; Mrs. John H. Ware, III and her sister, Mrs. E. M. Applebaugh, friends in their teens of former trustee Daniel T. V. Huntoon; and Mrs. H. Rohs Arlinghaus, daughter of former trustee John P. B. Sinkler, have supplied biographical details.

Sir Victor Johnson, Bart., of Sussex, England, generously enabled us to obtain color photographs of the portraits of Rebecca Franks Johnson and her husband, Sir Henry Johnson, and to examine the Johnson family papers; while Michael and Evangeline Hunter-Jones, of London, have been invaluable in other matters in England. Mrs. James Pritchard, of Haverford, through her friend Mrs. Ruth Buxton, of Bath, England, unraveled the mystery of Rebecca Franks Johnson's grave at the church of St. Michael with St. Paul—after our continued efforts in Bath had proved unsuccessful.

We here express our sincere appreciation to all those named above and to those others who have given of their time, materials, and knowledge for this book.

Preface

By the simple stroke of her pen in 1921 Naomi Wood integrated for the indefinite future the lives of countless persons concerned in some way with her Collection or with Woodford Mansion.

There are the many craftsmen and artists who created the furnishings and equipage which she and her trustees have assembled into one Collection bearing her name; and the many experts from here and abroad who have freely shared their knowledge and suggestions concerning that Collection.

Then there are the few of wide importance in their day who built and those who owned Woodford, their families and helpers who lived there, the generations of Fairmount Park employees who worked in and from it, the many who were tried, fined and detained there, and the restorers who strengthened, preserved and unobtrusively modernized the fabric of the structure.

There are, as well, those who have and who will administer her Trust, those who guide visitors through the Collection, and the visitors who derive from the mansion a realization of beauty in early home life and an inspiration for higher achievement in their own lives.

In leaving her estate to display an example of "Colonial household gear," Miss Wood hoped to inspire those who would follow after her by showing the kind of life lived here by self-reliant men and women. Those early owners of homes like Woodford, scattered down the east coast—with the frontier only a hard horseback ride away—were builders not only in brick and mortar but builders of the social fabric of our country. Venturing, enterprising, often acting with the public good in mind, they combined ideals with practicality. Their values were sound—above all the high value they assigned to freedom. Especially was this so in Philadelphia and Pennsylvania, where three hundred years ago William Penn voiced and brought into practice the principle of religious freedom and that principle nurtured his colony until Philadelphia became the largest of the Colonial cities. Visitors must go away remembering that life here was and is free and that it will take some sacrifice to keep it that way. Those who came early from Europe found they could exercise their free choice of a livelihood and pursue the life they wished in America; and so can today's arrivals. It was the free worker who took pride in his work and the purchaser who appreciated it who created what the visitor sees in both the house and the Collection.

Neither can function without the other. The house has a clearly felt character, elegance and enduring strength. The Collection is the perfect garment to clothe the mansion with all the "household gear"—the utilitarian as well as the purely decorative—which helps make a house a home. The combined Collection and mansion has completed its fifty-first year and became in 1978 a National Historic Landmark by designation of the United States Department of the Interior.

Aesthetically, the visitor views the zenith of Philadelphia, and indeed early American, decorative arts and house furnishings. When he leaves the Collection with an understanding of American life as it was actually lived in seaboard cities at the time our country was built, he will have a deeper realization of what was won for us all when freedom triumphed over colonialism.

Miss Naomi Wood's Collection was a venture in things. Her will and its gift to the public remain a venture in faith.

Contents

Preface		7
I	*Naomi Wood and Her Plan*	11
II	*William Coleman, Originator of Woodford*	24
III	*Alexander Barclay, His Majesty's Comptroller of the Port of Philadelphia*	34
IV	*David Franks, Loyalist Who Completed Woodford*	47
V	*Rebecca Franks, Tory Belle*	68
VI	*Thomas Paschall, David Hayfield Conyngham, William Lewis*	85
VII	*Seventy-Five Years of Wharton Family Ownership*	93
VIII	*The Fairmount Park Period*	101
IX	*The First Fifty Years of The Naomi Wood Collection*	112
X	*The Naomi Wood Collection Today*	128
XI	*Architectural Development of Woodford Mansion*	136
Notes		150

Naomi Wood, photographed in Providence, Rhode Island

I
Naomi Wood
and Her Plan

In the early years of the twentieth century Naomi Wood conceived a project to serve the public both educationally and artistically, which became the main interest of her life, a source of study, collecting and planning. Her vision finally materialized with the aid of her friend Daniel T. V. Huntoon after her death in 1926. The story of the Naomi Wood Collection and how Mr. Huntoon brought it to be displayed at Woodford Mansion is an exciting combination of careful planning and chance. Miss Wood never knew that Woodford and Philadelphia's Fairmount Park would be the site of her benefaction. The similarity of her name with that of the mansion is purely coincidental.

Naomi Wood was born at 1322 Chestnut Street, Philadelphia, on June 12, 1871. Her grandfather, David Wood, had come to the city from New England and bought the building where she began life, which stood on one of Philadelphia's major arteries and very near another, Broad Street. Naomi's father, Caleb, Jr. and his bride lived there during the early years of their marriage, with Naomi's grandparents. Caleb, Jr. kept a store on the ground floor for "ladies' and children's furnishing goods." He died in 1897, when Naomi was twenty-six. After that the property was rented out for investment. In 1920 a good offer was made for it and it was sold for a substantial amount, for it stood on the south side of the street immediately across from the monumental new Wanamaker store. The proceeds were reinvested and created the foundation for the Naomi Wood estate.

Miss Wood was an attractive young woman. A cousin described her as "very highly educated. She had a determined mind, and [was] quick in making decisions—a person well able to hold her own under any and all conditions. She was not of the sensational type, but in manner and general appearance a little out of the ordinary, a rich man's only child whose hobby was antique furniture, etc. and financially able to satisfy her desire and efforts on this score."[1]

It was quite usual at that time for an only daughter to remain a companion to her widowed mother. Naomi never married. She lived with her mother in various cities until the latter died in 1923.

Naomi had begun acquiring antiques before 1905, when they were living in Ardmore, Pennsylvania, less than ten miles from the center of Philadelphia and one of its "main line" western suburbs. By that year she had formed the idea of displaying what she had collected in a home to be designed and built largely for that purpose. She was attracted to the hilly, wooded country surrounding Paoli, twelve miles further west. Title was taken in her mother's

Naomi Wood's family home and birthplace Chestnut Street, Philadelphia

**Early portion of Naomi Wood's Collection
at Paoli House   Circa 1909**

name to a lot of substantial size, less than a mile from the Paoli railroad station,[2] and upon it a house was designed and erected in Dutch Colonial style specifically for the needs of Naomi and her mother. The house remains a handsome residence today. The collection was displayed in the living room, hallway and dining room which comprised the first floor except for the kitchen, and in her mother's and her bedrooms and a connecting study which comprised the second floor except for servants' quarters. Both the house and the collection were the subject of the lead article in the October, 1909 issue of the magazine *Philadelphia Suburban Life*.[3]

In the planning of the house and the installation of the antiques in it Miss Wood was assisted by her friend Daniel T. V. Huntoon, who was to play a central part in the establishment of the Naomi Wood Collection at Woodford Mansion after her death. A year older than Naomi, he had been brought up in Canton, Massachusetts, in strict New England fashion, the grandson of a Unitarian Minister, Benjamin Huntoon. His family had a strong cultural interest in old New England. His father wrote the history of the town of Canton. Growing up in this atmosphere, Daniel began quite early to collect: furniture and household articles first; later pewter, prints and silhouettes; and quite late in life, silver. He inherited beautiful old family pieces from his grandfather a few of which are a part of the Collection at Woodford today.[4]

At about the year 1900 Daniel Huntoon resigned as President of a business he had operated and came to Philadelphia. He joined in establishing there the investment brokerage firm of Reed and Huntoon. This was dissolved after World War I. Thereafter he continued his part of it as Huntoon & Co. and remained a resident of Philadelphia until his death. He was buying antiques from Philadelphia dealers not later than 1904 and furnished his business office with early American furniture, prints and silhouettes.

Sharing a common interest, he and Naomi Wood became good friends. Her Paoli house was early evidence of the length to which her enthusiasm for Americana carried her. Daniel Huntoon's business duties permitted him to spend substantial time at the Paoli house, where he placed some of his own basic pieces to round out the display.

Despite the designing, building and furnishing of a wholly new house in Paoli, it was sold only four years later in 1912, Mrs. Wood stating that she was a resident of Gloucester, Massachusetts, where she and Naomi then had a summer home.[5] An advertisement for the sale stated provocatively that "The owner and occupant has a satisfactory reason for selling, and the reason means a 20% saving to the purchaser."[6]

Whatever the reason for abandoning the Paoli house, furnishing that house with a collection of antiques, including some of Mr. Huntoon's pieces, served an exceptional purpose: Naomi and he determined to pool their collections and place them in a Colonial house sufficiently important to open as a museum for the public. Miss Wood had the means to buy and endow; he already had many of the large furniture pieces and some of the household equipment necessary to a furnished Colonial home. A surviving copy of a codicil not later than 1913 to her 1910 will shows that the whole project had already been outlined in 1910 in the same general terms as those later contained in her final will of 1921.[7]

With birth of the new and to-become-final objective, the purchase of antiques accelerated. Naomi and her mother's home at East Gloucester served as a headquarters for antiquing. Naomi was busy gathering both information and acquisitions. She studied and made notes of various items at the Gardiner Museum at Brookline, just outside Boston, in her handwritten notebook begun in 1911. She toured the surrounding country to make purchases from dealers not only in Boston but in smaller centers ranging from Ipswich and Salem to Concord and Wellesley Hills.[8] After her death her cousin stated that she thought Naomi's antiques had been "largely secured in New England territory.[9] Mr. Huntoon took summer quarters in an inn nearby and was available for trips, opinions and advice. They became friends of such experts as Wallace Nutting and Luke V. Lockwood, each the author of books on antiques.

Another activity in New England was the search for the perfect house, which would be "open for public inspection," in which to display the collection. In a petition filed with the court after her death in 1926, Mr. Huntoon stated that he and Miss Wood had visited many homes during a period of twenty-five years in the search for a suitable repository, particularly in New England, but that it had appeared to them that there was already an adequate number of house museums established and functioning in that area.[10]

Miss Wood did not desert Philadelphia, however. She still lived there at times with her mother in hotel apartments, although she also lived in like quarters in New York and Washington. Numerous antique dealers in Philadelphia and the old communities in the surrounding area, such as Ambler, West Chester and Pottstown, made sales to Miss Wood. Her constant and continuing activities led her also to attend auctions and to acquire items at "private sale" and by gift. At museums she compared antique items on display with her own of the same kind. Her notebook refers to a green satin cover, saying "almost similar pattern in Memorial Hall" (the former art gallery of the Centennial in Fairmount Park and until about 1928 the home of the City's museum of art). Her notes included many pen and ink drawings illustrating details of furniture styles, methods of preserving furniture, and its upkeep — even extending to drawings of such subjects as different styles of brass drawer pulls.

By this time, and perhaps much earlier, Mr. Huntoon was managing Miss Wood's and her mother's business and financial affairs, always with the highest integrity. In 1920 he was directly involved with the sale of the Wood family property on Chestnut

Street in Philadelphia, acting under her power of attorney. She wrote to the Girard Trust Company in that matter that "Mr. Huntoon is to be considered as our friend and representative regardless of the fact that he has a client who wishes to buy—I know Mr. Huntoon's absolute conscientiousness." In his accounting for his part in another transaction concerning the property he wrote that it "was conducted by me without profit in the interest of Miss Naomi Wood." Again in 1923 she notified Huntoon & Co. that she was appointing the Girard Trust Company as her agent "in compliance with Mr. Huntoon's request".[11] This action set the stage for the trust company's involvement as her corporate executor and trustee in the final establishment of her collection.

In her later years Naomi's collecting interests expanded somewhat, but she did not change her basic plan for a public museum exhibition. She had been buying books as early as 1906; now her sources broadened. In 1924 she traveled to Paris, where books were delivered to her by Quaritch of London.[12] During these last years she also developed an interest in Continental and Far Eastern antiques. While living with her mother in New York from 1921 to 1923 she bought numerous Chinese works of art, Hindu jewelry

Naomi Wood at her East Gloucester, Massachusetts, summer home

and antique Italian and Spanish furniture. The intellectual side of her pursuits remained strong. A note refers to "S's chain — Hindu — Metropolitan Museum same pattern *precisely,*" and to her using as a reference "Indian Jewelry of Historic Types XVII to XIX Centuries."

The death of her mother in 1923 found Naomi's collection partially in storage at East Gloucester and elsewhere. This loss impelled her to make a detailed review and obtain a better perspective for carrying out her own plan. Various inventories were prepared, such as one devoted solely to her items in Massachusetts, and another to articles she had disposed of.[13] She had been augmenting and upgrading, a practice she directed by her will be continued after her death.

In 1926, while a resident of Washington, D.C., Miss Wood traveled to England, where she died at the Royal Clarence Hotel in the cathedral close of Exeter on June 21. Her Bible had been inscribed "Given to myself as one who believes in God and Righteousness, recognizing no one creed as superior to another but rather believing in the superiority of daily practice as opposed to Sunday pretensions." She was only fifty-five. She had named

Daniel Huntoon her individual executor and trustee. He was in the United States at the time of her death, and guided the settlement of the financial side of her estate in Washington.

Next came the task for Mr. Huntoon and the trust company as executors and trustees to assemble Miss Wood's Collection into the public display which her will ordained. Clearly Mr. Huntoon had agreed to be the guiding spirit in this. She placed directly upon him the full responsibility for accomplishing it. The Will[14] directed that he begin by taking over "as soon as possible" all the house furnishings stored in the Gloucester area and at her New York apartment. She assured that he would be financially able to give extensive time to her project by setting up payment of an annual sum to him, stating "I wish my recognition of my friend, Daniel T. V. Huntoon's, interest in my welfare through the courses of many troublous years, to become effective immediately." Further, she left to him the income of a separate fund to "be invested, reinvested and kept invested in such securities as the said Daniel T. V. Huntoon in his sole discretion shall direct" and gave him the right to occupy free of rent, and the duty to furnish and equip, the house to be purchased by her estate and maintained as an "illustration of Colonial household gear." This was the position he had occupied as early as 1910 under her superseded will of that year.

The first required step was to select the place in which the Collection would be exhibited to the public. Reflecting the lack of a decision on this point, the will directed, as it had in 1910, that $50,000 be used to purchase such a house, without designating even in what state it would lie.

However, both Mr. Huntoon and the trust company were in Philadelphia; Miss Wood had been born there and had lived there for lengthy periods; the city had a rich Colonial background; and New England had been discarded as a proper site. Then, too, Miss Wood's and Mr. Huntoon's discussions had noted that houses in rural areas, even if architecturally of the proper age and style to house the collection, would be undesirable because of their location "in isolated places where a historic collection would be lost as a public benefit."[15]

In conjunction with these factors, Miss Wood's death occurred just at the time that a broad civic effort was commencing in Philadelphia for restoring and opening for public visitation the eighteenth and nineteenth century mansions in Fairmount Park.

The press reported early in 1926 that "A restorations programme for the historic mansions and colonial houses built many years ago in Fairmount Park has been undertaken by the Commissioners of Fairmount Park, the annual report of Chief Engineer Alan Corson discloses . . . Of all such mansions and estates . . . possibly only two . . . [Egglesfield and Lansdowne] have been removed. The others . . . have been preserved carefully by the Park Commissioners. Chief Corson, in his report, states this work of maintenance and restoration has been taking on new impetus. The old mansions are being kept, or being returned, to their original architectural state."[16] When it came to details, however, the report showed that restoration "during the past year" in the East Park had extended only to the mansion known as Lemon Hill. Work on another, Mount Pleasant, had commenced earlier by the Pennsylvania Museum with the aid of a substantial private contribution.

It happened that in 1925 Fiske Kimball, later Director of the new Philadelphia Museum of Art, had been brought by Eli Kirk Price, President of the Fairmount Park Commission, on a temporary visit from his museum employment in New York City with the idea that he might become the Director. The new museum was under construction on the site of the old reservoirs in the earliest part of Fairmount Park. Where might Dr. Kimball be housed if he were to be employed?

Kimball was taken by automobile to Mt. Pleasant, rather near the Museum, and became engaged in conversation with his guides, Park Superintendent Alan Corson and his assistant, Russell Thayer Vogdes, on the subject of the wonders of the group of Fairmount Park mansion houses.[17] Kimball was hired, and through the offices of Mr. Price was installed in Mount Pleasant. Kimball quickly discerned that from the plateau of the new museum another old Park house, considerably closer, could be seen through the trees. He completed its restoration to his own taste and moved into Lemon Hill Mansion in the spring of 1926. This left Mount Pleasant unoccupied. A citizens group undertook to remedy this with furnishings loaned from the Pennsylvania Museum and opened Mount Pleasant to the public at about July 4, 1926. The restoration movement was now fairly launched[18] with the hearty support of Mr. Price, and just at the time of Naomi Wood's death in June.

The minutes of the Fairmount Park Commission record that at its meeting in March, 1927 a communication was received from Mr.

Huntoon requesting that Woodford Mansion, in the East Park, be given over to the trust established by Miss Wood's will, in order that her Collection could be installed for public display.[19] This was a fine old house of formal Georgian character dating from 1756-1757, which had become the headquarters of the Fairmount Park Guard of mounted police. As long ago as 1898 the press had reported that of thirty-five old mansions and farm houses in the Park at that time, Woodford was "a perfect type of an old English manor house, and has been fortunately free from the desecration of the meddling Colonial 'restorer.' It looks just as it did fifty years ago."[20] Now it was stated that Miss Wood's estate had been offered its choice of a large number of the mansions.[21] But because the Collection, known in every detail to Mr. Huntoon, was very largely devoted to the earlier styles and would best be installed in a Georgian mansion, and because Mount Pleasant had already been open to the public for several months, Woodford was the obvious choice. A chance meeting with Mr. Price had led to his "prevailing upon" Huntoon to give Philadelphia first consideration in making his selection and to choose one of the historic mansions in Fairmount Park.[22] Hence the written formal request, the only item in the minutes.

They further show only that the application was referred to the Committee on Superintendence. But Mr. Price was Chairman of that Committee as well as President of the Commission. A notation written later by Mr. Huntoon states that Mr. Price was "instrumental in having the Estate of Naomi Wood restore and furnish Woodford Mansion." Effingham B. Morris, President of the corporate trustee, was also a man of wide influence who, according to Mr. Huntoon, "assisted in obtaining Woodford Mansion for the housing of Miss Wood's collection."[23]

At the July, 1927 meeting of the Commissioners the decision was recorded to commit Woodford to the care of the Naomi Wood trustees for an indefinite period, permitting them to make alterations "as may be necessary to restore it as nearly as possible to the condition at the close of the Colonial period," subject to approval of all plans by the Commissioners. At this same meeting, Chief Engineer Corson was directed to transfer the headquarters of the Park Guard as soon as possible from Woodford to the old Carousel building in the West Park.[24]

But all the activity in Philadelphia was insufficient to meet the

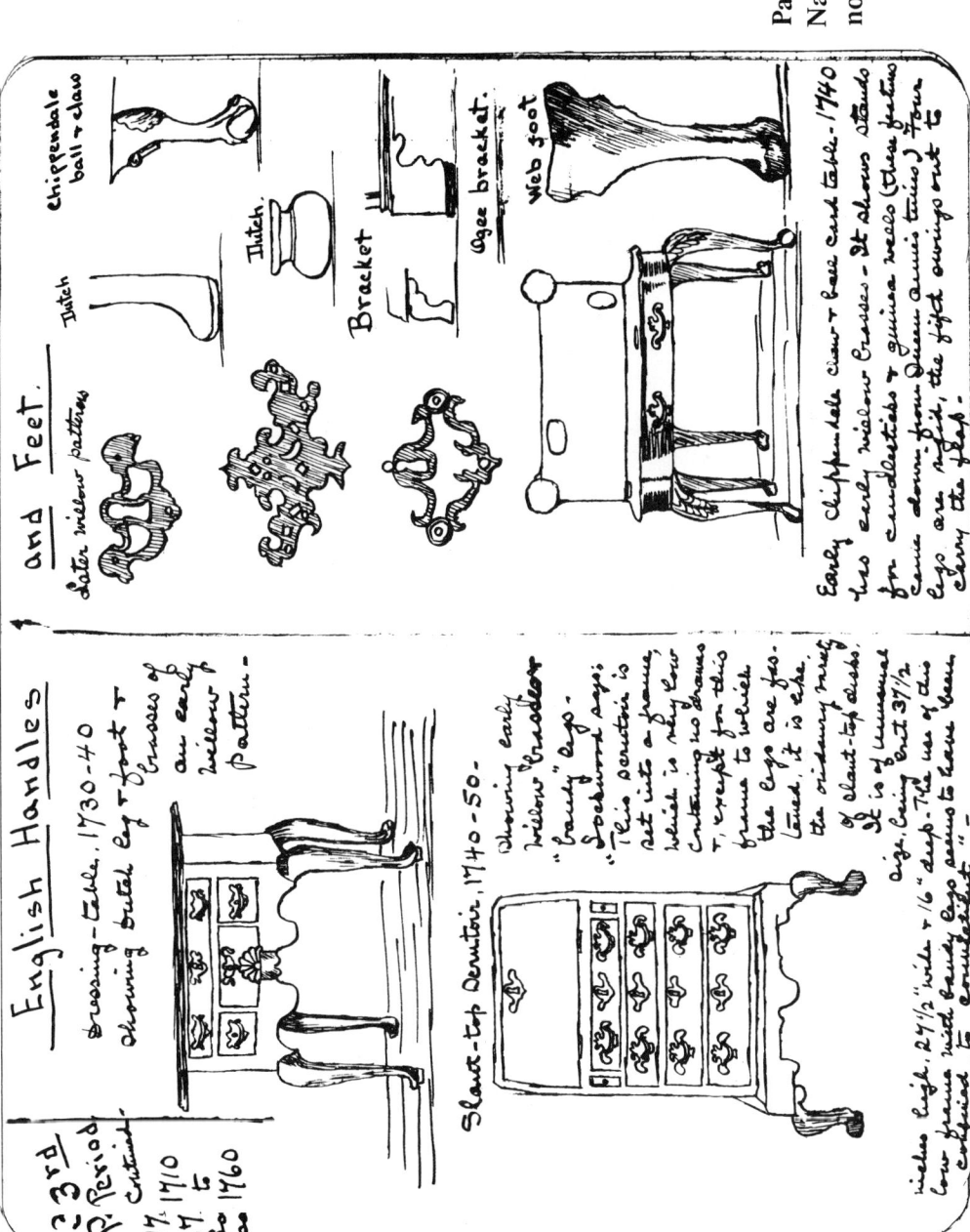

Pages from Naomi Wood's notebook

**Daniel T.V. Huntoon during his Trusteeship
1927 – 1943**

legal requirements. The approval of the court in Washington was necessary. In their petition to it, filed in June, the executors recited that since Miss Wood's death they had inspected numerous Colonial houses "in various localities"; that the majority of them were located in remote sections such as would defeat Miss Wood's purpose; and that since January, 1927 they had been attempting to obtain from the City of Philadelphia "the indefinite use of a splendid example of a Colonial house, which said house your petitioners are of the opinion is admirably suited for the purposes specified in the will. The said house is of pre-revolutionary construction, having been built between the years 1750 and 1770, constructed of English brick on true Colonial lines; and a careful inspection of the house leads your petitioners to believe that practically no changes have been made in the construction of the house since its final completion. The interior moldings, doors, stairways and windows are [in] an excellent state of preservation showing only very slight modification from the original. The house in question is situated in Fairmount Park in the City of Philadelphia, Pennsylvania, very near to one of the main entrances to the Park and within 1,000 feet of trolley and bus lines, requiring only 15 minutes ride from the center of the City of Philadelphia . . . The said house is at the present time used as a guard house for the officers and men who police Fairmount Park."[25]

The court permitted the trustees to hold against possible future use for her purpose the $50,000 Miss Wood had earmarked for the purchase of a house, and at the same time to take other funds from the estate to pay for the restoration of Woodford.[26] Now it was definite that Miss Wood's plan would bring a valuable new asset to Philadelphia and to the public everywhere. The mansion would be furnished with an outstanding collection, and the home to be recreated was that of men and women important in the early development of Pennsylvania and the United States. The story of their building and living at Woodford shows how they left their mark upon it, creating a repository worthy in combination with the Collection.

Naomi Wood,—

William Coleman, Originator of Woodford

Summer homes along the Schuylkill River were early found desirable by wealthy and influential Colonial Philadelphians as a way of escaping the heat and odors of the largest and most important city in the Colonies.[1] Edging ever closer to the river as its distance from the city increased was an old Indian trail that led from the northern side of the city. The Wissahickon Road, as it was known, went northwest. At the mouth of the Wissahickon Creek it came alongside the river, then mounted the great ridge lying to the east of it through present-day Roxborough. The then undammed Schuylkill flowed rapidly down through today's Fairmount Park to pass almost two miles west of the infant city. The river itself on the one hand, and the Wissahickon Road on another, formed with the northern boundary of the city a giant triangular area which in the early days was farmed.

The land along the east side of the Schuylkill in this area passed through the inevitable process of breakdown into ever smaller holdings. One piece of two hundred acres was carved out of the forest by a grant from William Penn to an Irish Quaker, Dennis Rotchford. After Rotchford's death, his widow sold it in 1693 to Thomas Shute for one hundred thirty pounds. Shute left it in 1748 to his son Joseph, upon his payment to the estate of nine hundred pounds; but Joseph declined, and the property was sold to Abel James, a prominent merchant. After another two years Joseph acquired title from James, now for a thousand pounds, but the place remained charged for the payment of debts and was put up for sale by the sheriff as property of the Thomas Shute estate.[2] This was farmland four miles from town on a bumpy dirt road. There were no purchasers. Next a piece of twenty-nine acres fronting on the Wissahickon Road was selected from the two hundred. It drew no buyers. A part of this small piece, being twelve acres fronting on the river side of the Wissahickon Road was put up for sheriff's sale at "John Biddle's House" (the Indian King Tavern on Market Street) in May, 1756[3] and found a taker in William Coleman. The deed was signed on July 19.[4] Coleman paid eight pounds per acre or ninety-six pounds for the whole.

He was no farmer, but rather a long-established merchant, a man of learning possessing collections of books and mathematical instruments, and a highly-respected judge. He lived in town, yet he saw the relative ease of reaching his new property by road. At the same time it lay within an easy walk of the river. Here he planned to build the first formal mansion in the area, as a retreat for summer use. He was married and childless, but he and his wife Hannah had raised her nephew, George Clymer, as their own from boyhood.

Judge Coleman was well acquainted with the new and handsome Georgian style of architecture which was coming into vogue locally for residences. It was but natural for his country seat to be built by a master carpenter to designs in that style selected from English pattern books. He and his architect-builder formulated a massive, rectangular one-story, two-bedroom main house of brick, with two smaller stone buildings of identical size to the rear. One of these contained four rooms for servants, the other a stable or chair-house.[5]

Coleman's material needs had been met from his earlier years spent as a merchant, an importer of dry goods when the desire for imports was strong. His father had been a Quaker "house carpenter" or builder, so Coleman undoubtedly knew the best builder-architects. By this time he was no longer a Quaker himself. He possessed ample wealth and could readily afford a carefully designed and solidly constructed set of buildings which would bring to his summer home along the Schuylkill greater amenities than those at his town house not far from the Delaware.

Coleman's Woodford, for so it came to be called, was the

retreat of a bookish man, fond of a quiet evening by a good fire, far from the cares of the city. His sunny parlor lay on the south side of the house, its handsome overmantel a constant joy. This room was separated by a classical arched hallway from two smaller bed chambers beneath which lay the kitchen in the basement. The "Tuscan" front door, a fine pedimented feature standing between engaged columns, was approached by railed soapstone steps. A massive bolt required no lock. The windows of the house were for the 1750s high and airy, as well as ample in number. A part of the outside brickwork was finished with alternating black brick headers. Coleman was more than comfortable in his new surroundings; he was dignified and uplifted by them.

Coleman came from families directly involved in the founding of the city. His mother remembered an infant Philadelphia. She had arrived as a child in 1683, within a year of the city's founding, and recalled that the then village "consisted of but three houses, and the other dwellings were caves" cut into the high bank of the Delaware along the waterfront.[6] She was Rebecca Bradford, eldest daughter of Thomas, another master carpenter on the Philadelphia scene. Her father had bought five hundred acres of land in the Province, and he sat on the Common Council of Philadelphia for fifteen years. The chief beneficiaries of his estate were Coleman's parents and their children.[7] This inheritance may have enabled William Coleman to start his own business as a merchant.

Although his father was one of the earliest members of the Carpenters' Company of Philadelphia,[8] Coleman did not follow his father's trade. His early employment as a merchant's clerk was a farsighted choice which led to wealth, a highly respected position in the community, and indeed, fame throughout the Province of Pennsylvania. He was a "doer," a mixture of one ambitious and active, yet always ready to give of his talents and wealth for the public good.

Coleman was already more than fifty, and one of the best known citizens of Philadelphia, when he built Woodford. In his chosen career he had had his own counting house for many years.[9] He had wide and desirable contacts. Many of them were developed from his far-ranging interest in civic endeavors and public improvements. He had long been one of the closest friends of Benjamin Franklin, who was just about his age. Franklin wrote in his autobiography that his friendship with Coleman had continued without interruption "upward of forty years."[10] It seems to have begun from Coleman's early interest in books, an uncommon attribute in those times for a busy merchant who was not one of the leisured class. As Franklin said, there was no good bookseller's shop in any of the colonies south of Boston; and in Philadelphia the printers were truly only stationers, selling almanacs, ballads and school books. Those who loved reading "were obliged to send for their books from England."[11] Coleman was one of these. A characteristic so notable as to be mentioned in his obituary was that he was "much pleased with Study and Retirement."[12]

Thus it was that as early as 1727 Coleman at twenty-three became a founding member of the first of many Philadelphia organizations which were the product of Franklin's sensitivity to public needs: the "Club of Mutual Improvement" or Junto. The Junto was a pooling of access to books and knowledge. Its membership was kept secret so as to avoid their being importuned by persons desiring its immediate advantages but lacking its peculiar qualifications. Meeting each Friday evening, it required every member in turn to produce one or more queries on points of morals, science, and politics which would be discussed by the membership. Every three months each member had to produce and read an essay of his own composition. Franklin characterized it as "the best school" of such subjects "as then existed in the province."[13]

From the Junto sprang the Library Company of Philadelphia, in 1731. Still in his twenties, Coleman was its first Treasurer; and he remained a director until several years after Woodford was erected.

On November 25, 1735 he and Hannah Fitzwater declared at Philadelphia Meeting their intentions of marriage; Hannah's parents and Coleman's mother being present gave their consent[14] (his father had died in 1731). Their engagement continued for two full years. The marriage allied Coleman with a strong and established Quaker family. Hannah was the granddaughter of Thomas Fitzwater who had come to Philadelphia on the ship *Welcome* with William Penn. Thomas embarked on the crossing with five members of his family, but only he, his two sons, Thomas and George, and his servant arrived in October, 1682. Smallpox claimed the lives of at least thirty of the voyagers including his wife Mary and another son and daughter.[15]

Thomas Fitzwater, Senior, took up land outside the city in what is now Montgomery County. The former Fitzwatertown and the present Fitzwatertown Road above Jenkintown stem from him. Fitzwater operated lime kilns on his land. Upon his petition Limekiln Pike was opened for the purpose of carrying lime from Fitzwatertown to Germantown. The kilns operated for more than a century and a half, but had disappeared by 1890.

Thomas Fitzwater was a member of the Provincial Assembly as early as 1683. Despite the distance involved in his own attendance, he voted to impose a fine of five shillings upon any member who should be absent for one whole meeting. He was described as an esteemed minister among the Quakers.

Hannah's father was Thomas' son, George Fitzwater, a successful merchant and an astute purchaser of land. His name appears in the records in carrying out the wills of numerous Quakers — evidence of the confidence in which he was held.[16]

In 1735 Hannah's sister Deborah married Captain Christopher Clymer, a sea captain plying to the West Indies, and a famous and successful privateersman.[17] He was a member of the Church of England and she was dismissed from Philadelphia Monthly Meeting for "marrying out of unity." Deborah died tragically in 1740 along with their baby daughter who was born less than a year after the arrival of their son, George. Captain Clymer also died, at only thirty-five, in July, 1746. At this point Hannah and William Coleman, who were childless, took their seven-year-old nephew into their home and brought him up as their own son.[18]

A few years earlier, and presumably because of Coleman's proficiency in mathematics, he had become one of the founders of the American Philosophical Society, the country's oldest and most distinguished scientific institution, formed in 1743 at Franklin's suggestion and another outgrowth of the Junto. He served as the first treasurer of the new society along with Franklin, its first secretary.[19] Later Coleman was one of those excited by the prospect of the transit of Venus, for which the Society erected an observatory in 1761 behind its building on State House (now Independence Hall) Square and conducted observations.

Although Hannah Coleman remained a Quaker for life, Coleman's participation in actions he considered necessary for Pennsylvania cost him his membership. In the spring of 1747 French and Spanish pirates appeared as marauders in Delaware Bay and caused great consternation to Philadelphia. They landed and carried off slaves and other property. Coleman's concern led him, with other merchants, to fit out a privateer, *The Warren*, to defend the bay and river by a month's cruise between the Virginia Capes and New Jersey. The Philadelphia Friends Meeting promptly called such conduct incompatible with proper Quaker tenets. Coleman, adhering to the view his principles required, was read out of Meeting.

The fitting out of *The Warren* and Coleman's leaving the Friends were tied in with Philadelphia's first sanctioned public lottery in 1748, Franklin's idea. With the approval of the Mayor and the Corporation of the city, Franklin ran off a thousand hand bills and printed ten thousand tickets for a lottery to cover the costs of building Philadelphia's first military defense, the Association Battery on the Delaware just below Old Swedes Church, outside the city proper. The city itself purchased two hundred tickets. Coleman was one of the managers of the scheme.[20] His group sent tickets to be sold in New York, New Jersey and Virginia. Almost all the tickets were disposed of within seven weeks time. The venture succeded largely because of Franklin's new pamphlet, *Plain Truth*, which included a number of Coleman's suggestions.

The drawings were held in February, 1748. Franklin won twelve pounds which he donated to the fund. With the lottery proceeds in hand, the managers selected the site for the Battery, ordered cannon from London, and in due course published a full accounting of expenses. The furor raised in the minds of the Philadelphia Monthly Meeting at these quasi-military, albeit defensive, activities was in Coleman's mind unjustified: he refused to acknowledge any error and indeed was joined in his thinking by no less a person than William Penn's secretary, James Logan, who is said to have invested two hundred and fifty pounds in the project.

This affair served to strengthen even more the friendship between Franklin and Coleman. Two years later, in June, 1750, Franklin drew his will, making his wife and son his executors but stating in it, "I desire my good friends Wm. Coleman and Philip Syng to give them from time to time their advice where it may be needful in the settlement of my affairs." Coleman was present at the signing and subscribed his name as a witness.[21]

It was an unspoken tribute to Coleman's sterling personal qualities that as a non-Quaker in the days when Philadelphia was very largely Quaker, his career prospered in many broader directions with his increasing maturity from this time forward. He shared Franklin's desire for a chartered educational institution. When in 1749 the great building erected on Fourth Street north of Market to accommodate Whitefield's preaching became available, Coleman joined in the effort to secure a charter for an Academy and College. He was one of its original trustees as well as their clerk and the subscriber of ten pounds to its purposes. He selected and ordered for the institution books, maps and instruments from abroad. He held office as its treasurer until his death. It later became the University of Pennsylvania.

During these years Coleman actively supported Dr. Bond's and Franklin's efforts to charter a hospital. In 1751 he signed a petition to the Assembly for this purpose, and he kept a tin hospital charity box in his house. The Pennsylvania Hospital was incorporated in 1751 and occupied the east wing of its present building in 1756. Coleman remembered it in his will.

Still another public-spirited venture with Franklin lay in forming the first company for insuring houses destroyed by fire. The Philadelphia Contributionship, known as the "Hand in Hand," was organized in 1752. Coleman was a founding director and set up its books.[22] Its insignia of four hands locked in mutual assistance, used on its fire marks in that same year, typified Coleman's attitude throughout his career.

In this same most active period when Coleman was approaching fifty and at the height of his powers, he commenced another and perhaps the most important of his public services. He was appointed a justice of the peace and judge of the county courts in 1751. This must have been a recognition of his judicious temperament and of the moral principles instilled in him by his Quaker upbringing; for as Franklin wrote, Coleman "had the coolest, clearest head, the best heart, and the exactest morals of almost any man I ever met with" and was one of Philadelphia's "ingenious men."[23] This from a man who not only was the preeminent statesman in establishing his own country but who dealt with the dominant political figures and the royalty of both France and England.

After some years of service in the lower judiciary, including the office of Presiding Justice of the Court of Quarter Sessions, Coleman was appointed by the Crown in 1758[24] as one of three judges of the Supreme Court of Pennsylvania. Here indeed was business of substance to be wrestled with in the seclusion of Woodford, his new country home. For Coleman was, with all the busy-ness of his mature life, a homebody in his inner heart — probably another ingrained trait from early days when he was imbued with the principles of William Penn. Writing to young James Pemberton, then in England, he voiced the philosophy he had already adopted: "As far as my Experience goes the greatest Happiness arises, not so much from new Scenes & Entertainments, as from a Steady quiet Mind & the Consciousness of doing right, and this Sort of Happiness a Man may find at Home."[25]

Coleman and his nephew seem to have been most congenial. George Clymer's first employment was in his uncle's counting house. Following his marriage to Elizabeth Meredith at Christ Church in March, 1765, he formed a firm with his wife's father and his new brother-in-law. Clymer quickly took up the political career which Coleman refused to more than skirt. Chief Judge Allen had strongly urged Coleman to become a candidate for the Provincial Assembly, but he had refused.[26] Clymer, however, became a delegate in 1775 to the Provincial Convention at Philadelphia which considered a constitution for the commonwealth; and in the fall of that year he was appointed to serve on the Committee of Safety. In 1776 he achieved lasting fame by signing the Declaration of Independence as a Pennsylvania delegate to the Continental Congress.

Coleman preferred public service of a local sort. In his mid-thirties he had first been elected a member of Philadelphia's Common Council. Here his frequent service in drafting messages to the Governor, resolutions and other formal papers had led to his being chosen Town Clerk of the Council after eight years of service. His resignation from this appointment in 1758 was probably due to his advancement to the Supreme Court but may have been inspired in part by the need to devote time to Woodford in that very year.

As a highly regarded member of the judiciary and a person with unusual qualifications in mathematics, Coleman was sought for one of his last services of the first magnitude. In 1761 he was appointed one of the Pennsylvania members of the Commission whose task was to adjust once and for all, the boundary between Pennsylvania and Maryland. Charles Mason and Jeremiah Dixon, expert English surveyors, were retained in 1763 jointly by William Penn's sons Thomas and Richard on the one hand and by Lord Baltimore on the other, physically to run and record the boundary.[27] But these new supervisory duties found Coleman, as he edged toward age sixty, beset with pain, for he was suffering from "the stone" and could not ride horseback. He administered the oath of fidelity in their performance to Mason and Dixon in the presence of the full Commission, was able to get to New Castle (then in Pennsylvania's Lower Counties but now part of Delaware) by boat, attended Commission meetings, and in his own hand prepared some of its reports. The successful completion of the survey in 1767 made the names of Mason and Dixon famous; the Commission certified their map of the boundary line late in 1768.[28] Before returning home the surveyors measured a degree of latitude in Pennsylvania and Maryland for the Royal Society, the results of that work eliciting articles in London's prestigious periodical, the *Gentleman's Magazine*, late in 1769.[29]

In 1766 Coleman's judicial responsibilities had increased as well, when he became second judge after serving as the junior member of the Supreme Court. On this occasion Franklin sent Coleman from London a gift of a copy of *The Principles of Equity* written by Lord Kames and published in 1760. It was also in the year of this promotion that he completed his new town house on the northeast corner of Second and Pine Streets in the city. It boasted a five-window front and, like Woodford, a great high portico and pediment and a garden.[30] Nicholas Wainwright has likened the nearby elegant Cadwalader house to Coleman's, saying Cadwalader's was "very much the same as Judge William Coleman's house, erected, probably by the Judge's close friend Samuel Rhoads."[31]

With no surcease from increasing problems of health, Coleman reached the point in 1768 where an operation on his person was the only hope for relief. With Franklin's assistance he sailed for England on March 31 on the brig *Nancy*,[32] five days after signing his will. In London he took a room in the same house in Craven Street where Franklin made his English home. Unfortunately the surgeon Coleman hoped to consult was on the continent; but the physicians advised that "he have the diseased part cut out," and the operation took place in June. Franklin and his landlady nursed Coleman back to health. Convalescence at Woodford must have been in Coleman's mind when he and Franklin discussed returning to Philadelphia in July; but this was not to be, and Coleman arrived alone in October.[33]

Although he had apparently recovered, he was met with successive new blows. His wife Hannah died in mid-November. On December 13 he signed a codicil to his will.[34] Now he was stricken again with such severity that he too died on January 11, 1769. He left the greatest part of his property to his nephew George Clymer, saying that he was persuaded that his wife would have done likewise because of her "great regard and particular affection" for him. Coleman's substantial personal estate included a library of three hundred fifteen volumes, and a case of mathematical instruments.[35] But he had directed that Woodford be sold.

Many years earlier, in 1728, as a young man, Coleman and another member of the Junto had supplied Franklin with the capital by which Franklin made himself sole proprietor of the *Pennsylvania Gazette,* Philadelphia's long-run newspaper. Now it was the *Gazette* which characterized Coleman as "a valuable and useful Citizen, and a Gentleman of great good Sense, and unblemished Virtue [who] possessed many social Virtues, and was ever fond of those Subjects, which were most likely to render him serviceable to his Neighbor. He was an able and an upright Judge, and in that Character gave the greatest Satisfaction to his Country. And we may say, with much Reason, that this Province has few such Men, and that few Men will be so much missed as Mr. Coleman."[36]

Although Franklin had asked his executors in his will to seek Coleman's advice, this was not to be. Franklin outlived Coleman more than twenty years; and indeed Coleman's mother survived him by more than a year to attain the age of ninety-two.

At Coleman's death Woodford was more than ten years old. It had already served one of the most influential men of the Province in his period and known Philadelphia's greatest citizen of all time, Dr. Franklin.

III
Alexander Barclay,
His Majesty's Comptroller of the Port of Philadelphia

William Coleman's will directed that Woodford should be sold "for the best price that can be gotten, to any person whatsoever" and that from the funds to be received from the sale, twenty pounds was to be distributed to each of his "grown negroes Azmin, Hagar and Philae"; five pounds were to be given with each of their children when they should be apprenticed to learn a trade; and all should be set free in due course.

In May, 1769 there appeared in the *Pennsylvania Gazette* an advertisement for the sale of Woodford at public auction which showed that Coleman had embellished his country estate in the usual fashion for summertime enjoyment by creating a garden and an orchard, well fenced—these in addition to the servants' or tenant house and the chair-house:

> THE COUNTRY SEAT late of William Coleman, Esq; within 4 Miles of the City of Philadelphia, on the West Side of Wissahickon Road, will be sold by public Vendue; it contains about 12 Acres, with a house of 3 Rooms on a Floor, finished in a neat Manner; an Out-house suitable for a Tenant, built of Stone, with 4 Fireplaces, 2 on each Floor, and a Cellar under the whole, a good Stone Chair-house and Stable, a handsome Garden, a thriving Orchard of good Apple Trees, and other Fruit, and a Well of excellent Water. The whole Place being under good Post and Rail and Pallisadoe Fence. The Sale to be on the Premises at 3 o'Clock on Thursday, the 18th of May inst. Several Years Credit will be allowed for the whole, if required, on giving sufficient Security, and paying Interest.[1]

The successful purchaser was Alexander Barclay, who held the Crown's appointment as "Comptroller of all the Rates and Duties and Impositions arising and growing due to his Majesty at Philadelphia." With his ownership Woodford entered into the circle of those in the Colony directly beholden to the sovereign who would be termed Loyalists or Tories when dissension, and later, revolution, came. And it was during the years that Barclay held his office that the first steps leading toward united Colonial action contrary to the interests of such persons were taken.

Barclay had come to Philadelphia in 1747 at age thirty-five as a local representative for his Uncle David's well-known firm of merchants in London.[2] He had a good education and was appointed by the Crown as Collector of Customs for Philadelphia in 1748, and promoted to Comptroller in 1751.[3] In his early years he had been commissioned in the Royal Army. He is said to have dissipated the fortune left him by his mother and to have led a dissolute life at that period — his will refers to his "natural daughter Sarah Thomson of London." But he appears to have settled down by the time of his arrival in America in a responsible capacity.

Alexander's grandfather had been one of the most influential and renowned of Quakers, Robert Barclay "the Apologist." Robert had become a convinced Quaker in 1667 at the age of nineteen, a year after *his* father had been converted to that faith.

Within ten years of his entering Quakerism Robert became involved in controversy about it and wrote two treatises. The second, "An Apology for the True Christian Divinity," published in 1676, made him the most eminent writer of the Quakers and is regarded as one of the most impressive theological works of the seventeenth century. He traveled to Holland and Germany with William Penn and George Fox; and he was imprisoned three times for his beliefs. He was treated with respect by Charles II and came to exercise much influence over the Duke of York, later King James II. As Robert said, "I love King James and wish him well." It was Robert who first took the family's affairs to America. As Duke of York, James issued a patent for the province of East New Jersey to twelve Quaker proprietors, and Barclay became Governor of the area from 1682 to 1688, serving by deputy. One of his brothers settled there; another died during his voyage to it.[4]

Alexander's father, David Barclay, was one of three brothers and four sisters, all of whom were alive fifty years after their father

Robert's death in 1690. This continuity was important in relationships with the Crown even though the Stewarts were ultimately replaced by the Georges of Hanover. David was a most successful Quaker banker and export merchant in London. In the 1750s he enjoyed a larger share of business with the mercantile community in Philadelphia than any other London firm.[5] With this accomplishment he was selected to look after matters still needing attention in William Penn's estate. The family firm he founded has continued through the centuries and is now Barclay's Bank, of London.[6]

There can be little doubt that the ongoing recognition of the Barclays by the King and Alexander's ready availability as a Philadelphia resident of a year's standing brought about his appointment as Collector at the age of thirty-six. In a letter to James Pemberton in Philadelphia toward the end of 1761, John Hunt of London wrote that he had been at David Barclay's when the King, Queen and royal family were there.[7] Thus the royal friendship with the Barclay family extended to George III who had taken the throne about a year earlier.

Alexander married Ann Hickman, a Quaker, in 1748. The daughter of Robert Hickman, a citizen and cabinet-maker of

F. Otto Haas

Ann Hickman Barclay
ca. 1748

London, and his wife Patience, she had arrived in Philadelphia a few years before Alexander to visit her uncle, John Hyatt, the High Sheriff of the city. Matching portraits of the young couple, still preserved, probably show them in Quaker garb and perhaps date from the time of their marriage. The Alexander Barclays were a lively pair, active in the social life of the city. But after only five years of marriage, Ann died, leaving her husband with two young children, Robert and Patience.

Alexander had lived on Union (now Delancey) Street near the New Market and the port, in a house which was also his office.[8] In 1758 he bought another house on the same street — a commodious one of Flemish-bond brick, the thirty-fifth house from the Delaware on the north side. It had been built by one of Philadelphia's highly qualified builder-architects, Samuel Rhoads,[9] with a two-story detached kitchen in back. Though the facade was simple, the house had a more elaborate interior, and Barclay furnished it well. A year later, after six years as a widower, on February 8, 1759 he brought to his new home a second wife, Rebecca Evans Robertson, widow of Peter Robertson, whom Alexander married at Christ Church.[10] She was both the daughter and granddaughter of earlier

F. Otto Haas

Alexander Barclay
ca. 1748

Collectors of Customs at Philadelphia.[11] It was this marriage that brought Woodford at the time of the Revolution to its zenith in the hands of Rebecca's brother-in-law, the prominent Loyalist David Franks; and it was Rebecca Barclay for whom her niece, Franks' famous and talented youngest daughter Rebecca, was named.

Barclay's advertisement in the *Pennsylvania Gazette* in 1761 required "all Captains and Commanders of Ships, to enter in and clear them out, according to law, at my office in Union Street, near the New Market."[12] Although with his official duties he combined those as a merchant in the business of David Barclay and Son, to the public it was as Comptroller that he was known. The small street beside his house became known as "Comptroller's Alley" (today Philip Street). A good part of the time of John Swift, his Collector from 1762, was spent in preventing the landing of cargoes without payment of duties, coping with altered clearance papers and other subterfuges.[13] Presumably these activities had occupied Barclay in that same appointment some years earlier, whereas, as Comptroller he now received the money, safeguarding it in what was called "the chest," and periodically forwarding it to his superiors in Boston, the Commissioners of His Majesty's Customs in America.

In 1763 the house lost an occupant when Barclay's son Robert was sent to London at the age of twelve to be educated and enter the family business in Cheapside.

Until about that year the collection of royal customs was regarded largely as a joke; but with the end of the French and Indian War, England needed much more revenue to support its troops stationed in the colonies for defense. One of the measures adopted was to tighten the enforcement of customs laws, while at the same time broadening the list of taxable items to which they applied and requiring clearance through British ports. Since one of the most odious new laws restricted the importing of molasses, the tax acts became known as the "Sugar Acts." The Colonies had a common cause for complaint and did so. But now Parliament passed the detested Stamp Act of 1765. The prospect of its becoming effective brought on the first meeting together or convention of the Colonies, held at New York.[14]

In Philadelphia Barclay was caught between his merchant friends and his father's firm's position, on the one hand, and his duties as a tax official appointed by the Lords of the Treasury on the other. He must have maintained a low profile as fellow merchants refused after a formal meeting to permit the stamps to be brought off shipboard; told John Hughes, who had been appointed Stamp Master for Pennsylvania, to resign; and, three hundred seventy-five strong, signed resolutions agreeing to import no goods or merchandise from England until the Stamp Act should be repealed.[15] That these were deadly serious acts is apparent from Hughes' recounting the threats made to him in a letter he sent on November 5, 1765 to Barclay, Barclay's Collector, and Thomas Graeme:

> ... a large number assembled at the State House where it was publicly said, as I am informed that if I did not immediately resign my office my House shou'd be gutted down and my substance destroy'd; by a note they at night sent me indulged me until 10 o'Clock the Monday morning following, to satisfy them, Whether I wou'd or not, resign my office as Stamp Distributor for this province.[16]

Hughes' written reply to this demand was equivocal and unpopular, but he never took possession of any of the stamps.

The Stamp Act was repealed,[17] but the unremitting efforts for more revenue in England led to new tensions. In 1767 duties were imposed on such articles as glass, paper and tea. The Pennsylvania Assembly at Philadelphia regarded this in the following year as "highly injurious to the rights of the people" and forwarded petitions to the King, the Peers and the Commons insisting on their rights as Englishmen.[18] More resolutions were adopted at public meetings. Some idea of the pressures on Barclay can be gained from an advertisement he and Swift inserted in the *Pennsylvania Gazette* on November 3, 1768 wherein the Commissioners of His Majesty's Customs offered the large reward of one hundred pounds for information as to a threatening letter left under the front door of their Philadelphia employee, the Searcher of the Customs, reading:

> Mr. Sheppard,
> I a few Days ago acquainted you, by Letter, that if you continued to execute your Office in Philadelphia, you would meet with Opposition, but it seems you have not regarded that Hint; I now again declare to you, that your Office is disagreeable to the People here, and that if you persist in acting in it, your Person, and Life, will be in great Danger; if you will continue in it, you must blame yourself for the Consequences; I wish you well in any other Employment. Saturday night.[19]

The year 1769 was no easier. At about April 1, Swift became embroiled in more trouble by seizing several pipes of Madeira wine which were landed without payment of custom. The seized goods were placed in storage along the waterfront; but at night a group of citizens stole up to the warehouse in boats, broke it open and carried the wine off. Although Swift was present, he was powerless. He was threatened and abused, and that same night the windows of his house were broken. A meeting of citizens at the Coffee House followed. The wines were returned to the government and several of the rioters were later tried and convicted.[20] The Quaker merchants took a more temperate approach to the problem this incident exemplified — by asking the Barclay firm in London to obtain relief from their grievances.

Under such circumstances the prospect of owning Woodford must have appeared an oasis of peace to Barclay. It was on May 18, 1769 that he took title to it for seven hundred forty-five pounds. But he gave a mortgage of five hundred pounds to Coleman's estate which was to be the cause of his family's losing the property later.[21] He ran a porch across the rear for the full width of forty-five feet, and it appears that he built an iron railing around the hipped roof;[22] but with only one child at home, there was no need to increase the size of the house.

Except as to tea, the new taxes were repealed in 1770. But soon after Barclay's purchase of Woodford another meeting had been called at the State House when a ship loaded with malt appeared, its importation being contrary to resolutions adopted earlier that year. The vessel was compelled to return to England with its cargo.[23] And in 1770, when trade was reopened, two lengthy local meetings were held on that question.[24] Barclay had been Comptroller for nearly twenty years by this time, but the continuous unrest and confrontations with the Crown, the source of his appointment, must have been wearing despite the retreat his new country house provided.

On January 12, 1771 Swift, now Barclay's Collector for some nine years, wrote to the Commissioners of Customs at Boston:

> It is with extreme concern that I am now to acquaint you that Mr. Barclay the Comptroller of this Port departed this life last night;—his disorder was the gout in his head. We acted together as officers of his Majesty's revenue at this port with the greatest of harmony for many years.

Swift recommended Lynford Lardner, uncle of the provincial Governor of Pennsylvania, as interim successor who, he wrote, "is one of the few persons in this City who have not joined with the multitude in giving all the opposition in their power to the measures of Government;—and he is not concern'd in trade."[25] A letter sent by Barclay's brothers David and John from London to his widow on March 6 mentioned receipt of a report of his "painful situation," the "severity of his disorder and the frequent attacks of it."[26] Doctors John Kearsley, Thomas Graeme, Phineas Bond and Cadwalader had been unable to save him.[27]

Barclay had been the first owner of Woodford to be caught up in what would grow to be a titanic conflict. This hastened his death but was not mentioned in the bland obituary published in Franklin's *Pennsylvania Gazette*. There he was described simply as "a Gentleman who was greatly esteemed by the Trading Part of this City as a good Officer, and by all his private Acquaintances as a benevolent and honest man . . ."[28]

Soon a new problem replaced the sadness of Barclay's death. He had left a financial muddle behind him. On April 3 his brothers wrote to Rebecca of Alexander's "involved affairs"; and his son Robert mentioned his family being "unhappily left encumbered and involved with numerous Charges." In the brothers' view:

> Woodford should be immediately disposed of, with such other Things as cannot be proper for the Situation of his Family in particular the carriage and Horses.

They offered to make advances for Rebecca and her stepdaughter Patience through Alexander's American executor and "trusty friend" Lardner.

The comment about Woodford was obviously made because Barclay had failed to pay when due his mortgage debt to the Coleman estate, which took the initiative by legal process. Once again the mansion was put up for auction, but this time for nonpayment of the debt. At the sale on June 21, 1771 David Franks gave the high bid of eight hundred eighty pounds. Since Franks' wife Margaret was the sister of Barclay's widow, Franks probably already knew the property during Barclay's short ownership. The Sheriff, Judah Foulke, who had deeded it to Barclay, sold on the premises at the same time "all the household furniture, garden implements, &c, belonging to the said place."[29] In writing to his stepmother Rebecca from England a month (August 22) after the deed was given, Barclay's son Robert apparently misunderstood the reason for sale by the Sheriff. Robert was twenty at the time and hence still under age:

> "That Woodford should be undersold on account of the Sheriffs being the only person to give a title surprises me not a little and I cannot well account for it, considering that in the common course of nature I should so soon be capable of giving a title myself, however as the thing is done there can be no remedy for it and we must be content."

The place was already being called "Woodford," both in letters in the family and in the formal account of Barclay's estate filed with the court which mentioned the sum which "Woodford estate sold for by execution."[30] It has commonly been assumed that the name was given in a combined reference to the surrounding wooded area and the nearby ford across the Schuylkill; but another possibility is that the name was copied from that of the family home of Barclay's close friend Lardner's sister, of *Woodford,* Epping Forest, Essex. She married Richard, son of William Penn and a joint Proprietor, with his brothers, of Pennsylvania.[31]

Whatever Rebecca was able to salvage locally from her husband's estate was increased in 1772. On August 27 of that year his brothers David and John informed her that young Robert, having come of age, had signed a bond to secure her an annuity of one hundred pounds a year as her husband had intended she should receive. She early expressed to Robert the fear that the creditors would take the Union Street townhouse and furniture, and indeed the Sheriff advertised the house for public sale. But Robert reassured her on the basis of statements by his uncles, and the Woodford sale price was sufficient to pay the debt to the Coleman estate in full. Rebecca lived at Union Street pursuant to her express desire until her death, supported by remittances from London.

Barclay left a will dating from 1764, prior to his acquiring Woodford, in which he appointed his brother James of London, a member of the family banking house, and Lardner of Philadelphia as his executors. The appraisal of Barclay's personal property, the sheriff also acting as one of the appraisers, listed quantities of furniture, silver and china in the Union Street house, plus at least thirty old prints, including one "Prospect of the City of Philadelphia." The appraisal also listed in detail the property at

Woodford and hence provides the only means of our knowing how the one-story mansion was used during the years preceding the Revolution.[32]

The Woodford "passage" or hallway had been used by the Barclays as a room for living, perhaps reading and chatting, rather than simply as a passageway to the porch. It contained "one large black walnut table," eight Windsor chairs, three rush-seated chairs and a couch. This accorded with the custom of the time.

The parlor, unchanged today, was furnished with a maple table holding a set of china, a mahogany card table, another black walnut table, a "Japand waiter" or serving table, additional "china and crockery" and nine "walnut leather bottom [i.e., seated] chairs." Thus the family used the parlor in part as a dining room—another common practice before the Revolution. The walls were furnished with "two gilt frame Sconces," perhaps similar to those in place today, four "brackets with images," a map of Pennsylvania and another unidentified print. The portraits of Barclay and his first wife remained at the townhouse.

Remembering that the present-day Woodford dining room was divided into two rooms, the inventory corroborates that the front one, the "chamber," was the bedroom. It contained a mahogany bedstead with red bolster and counterpane and blue and white bed curtains. It was also fitted with a dressing table and a mahogany book case, as well as fireplace accessories and "one spy glass." In "the little Back Room," truly a small one, were a pine bedstead and a walnut couch, perhaps used by Barclay's daughter Patience, still in her teens. However, the garret, plastered when built by Coleman, was fitted up with additional bedroom furniture. Such was Woodford in January, 1771.

Young Robert had written from London shortly after his father's death that his uncles felt "the appropriation of the furniture should be deferred till I am of age." Rebecca wanted him to come to Philadelphia promptly; but his letters show that only in 1773, at age twenty-two, did he return to America with a letter of introduction to James Pemberton stating that Robert "has a strong inclination to see once more his native country." While here, he took a lengthy trip to Niagara Falls and Indian country. His return to England was deferred until the Fall of 1774 by business in New York for the family firm. In 1775 he wrote to his stepmother, "I assure you I entertain a very great partiality for America, and I shall never cease to remember with singular delight the happiness my late Tour afforded me."[33]

Unlike his father as a young man, Robert was very steady and worked hard to move forward in his career as a merchant. He was solicitous of both Rebecca, whom he invariably addressed as his mother, and his younger sister. After the death of his grandfather David, founder of the family firm, his uncles continued it, and Robert wrote in January, 1773 "my uncles have taken me into partnership with themselves under the firm name of David and John Barclay & Co." In a letter introducing Robert to William Logan in Philadelphia, Robert's uncle David said he was induced "to part with him at a Time, that he is now becoming exceedingly useful—as this youth leaves with a Character that but few at his years have attained." By 1775 in a letter to Rebecca he was "thy valuable son."[34]

As the Revolution approached, David tried to sound a cautionary note for those in America:

> Opposition to despotism many approve, [but] *outrage* and every act that may be considered *Rebellion* should be prevented.

He saw matters in February, 1775 as at a "critical Conjuncture" but still thought British strictures could be limited to the Massachusetts Bay colony and clung to the idea of reconciliation. Robert was busy with both sides of the Atlantic. His uncle David had retired at the end of 1774; the firm now operated under the name John and Robert Barclay. In 1775 Robert married his cousin Rachel Gurney of Norwich, a Friend. But by September he had to report to his stepmother that "all resources from Trade are entirely clos'd."[35]

Robert's sister Patience had proved a problem from the time she reached maturity. At first it was that she and her stepmother were at odds, and Patience had little financial support. Robert's uncles directed by letter shortly after their brother's death that Patience be moved to a separate house, but this did not occur. Robert relayed their thought that in any case Rebecca should "settle herself pretty much independently" because Patience's stay would be uncertain "either thro Marriage or Removal." An allowance was set up from London for her "so long as she continues to behave herself consistent with the rules of Propriety."[36]

By January, 1773 Robert was referring to "my sister's imprudent Marriage" to Joseph Worrell. Robert expressed pleasure that they "have no thoughts of settling in Phila as that would lead them into a more expensive method of living than they can well afford." They set up housekeeping in Trenton, New Jersey, but soon Patience became a widow. In September, 1775 Robert wrote that her coming to London would "not prove agreeable to her friends here." At the end of the year he was afraid that "the horrid din of War" might approach Philadelphia and thought she should retire to "Easton or some other inland Town." Next Robert's uncles relented and offered Patience a passage to London, only to find, as Robert reported, that she rejected it, "preferring America to any village in this land."[37] This refusal may have been due to her relationship with Reynold Keen, a Philadelphia alderman and church warden of Old Swedes, whom she married on June 6, 1780, Bishop White officiating. But she died on January 4, 1781, in her twenty-ninth year, childless.[38]

Robert continued to write his stepmother at every opportunity during the War, when the packet boats were very few. Late in 1775 she was advised to move to the country, but not to Trenton because it was on the "Great Road to New York." In March, 1776 he again expressed concern for his mother's safety if Philadelphia should be attacked, as he thought probable, and begged her to send her most valuable effects out of the city to a safe place, "especially the Pictures of my honour'd and dear Father and Mother," and that she herself take refuge in Lancaster.[39] On November 4, 1777 "advices have just reach'd us that Phila is once more dependent on this government" [i.e., occupied by the British Army], and he expressed the ardent wish that "it may produce every good effect of a permanent tranquility." In January, 1778, during the occupation, he had just heard "of the Rivers being open'd [i.e., the reduction of Fort Mifflin by the British in November] and the passage clear," which he hoped would give Rebecca "constant and plentiful supplies of provisions, and that the formidable army you now have will preserve you in peace." However, Howe and the Army withdrew voluntarily in June.

Robert was still writing to Rebecca in 1783, the year of the peace. With her death in the following year his last immediate family connection with Woodford and America ended. He had now moved to Clapham outside London,[40] and there his life took a new turn which absorbed most of his energies. He became fascinated with botany and opened a correspondence with noted botanists in the new United States by which he secured many specimens for his collection. Through his uncle David, he learned of the availability of the Anchor Brewery which had been owned by a good friend of Dr. Samuel Johnson, Henry Thrale. Robert and others, including his uncle, formed a partnership and bought it. This lucky purchase made him immensely wealthy and permitted him to retire from his business.[41] He first rented and later bought an estate of some seven hundred acres, Bury Hill, where he formed a botanical garden, built a hothouse for his exotic plants, and even had an artist available at all times to draw the blossoms and make the drawings available to botanical journals for publication. He became a foreign member of the American Philosophical Society. The *Gentleman's Magazine* of London reported his death in 1830, long after Woodford's zenith during the Revolution.[42]

Alexander Barclay, who of the early owners held the title to Woodford for the shortest time, nevertheless has one distinction not accorded to any other of its owners and indeed to few, if any, others. His country house lives on, furnished with the Naomi Wood Collection. His town house at Delancey and Philip Streets also continues, in private ownership. The survival of both the pre-Revolutionary town house and the pre-Revolutionary country seat of the same person appears unique in the Philadelphia area and the sole, or one of the few, such remaining combinations in the United States.

IV

David Franks,
Loyalist Who Completed Woodford

David Franks was well schooled in the ways of the world. He probably regarded the sheriff's auction sale in the Barclay estate as the best way of fixing the true value of Woodford at the time of his purchase—particularly since it avoided any need to bargain within the family with his wife's younger sister whom he wanted to help. His daughter Polly was now twenty-three; his son Moses eighteen; and his daughter Rebecca, namesake of Rebecca Barclay, an enchanting young girl of thirteen.[1] This was the family who occupied Woodford.

David Franks is the person responsible for Woodford Mansion as it stands today, and the mansion is furnished in the period of its occupancy by the Franks family. He bought the house at the height of his powers and position. His fascinating career was one of great success in the Colonial period of our country, until his entire position, financial, family and social, was swept away, in his mid-fifties, by the Revolutionary War. He was a man of true integrity which in the first instance was instilled by his mother Abigail Levy Franks. Though Abigail lived in New York, her aspirations and her cultural interests were colored largely by England.[2] Many were her letters to her children when they were scattered from her. In May, 1733 she wrote to her son Naphtali, who lived in London, "I think its [to be really sincere] the greatest happyness a Person Can Injoy Next to the Haveing a good Conscience for As Addison Says A good Conscience is to the Soul what health is to the body."[3] She was a well-read person who in another letter reported that her receipt of a catalogue of books "Gave me the Pleassure that good Authors Genrely Infuse to a mind Inclined to books. I could with Vast Pleassure Imploy three hours of the 24 from my Family Affairs to be diping in a good Author."[4]

She was also astute in judging personal qualities. After her son David had gone to Boston in 1735 but decided he would prefer Philadelphia she wrote, "I believe he will be Very Indefatigable in business. He has not that Sprightly Genius that the rest have but I dare Say he never will be guilty of a mean base Action and Is Very well liked by all he Converses with. Neither does he Drink or Game. He has a Great mind to Come to London I Should think if he went there and Soe from thence to Philadelphia but I leave it intirely to your management."[5] David later went to London, but under totally different circumstances than those she envisioned.

The Franks family itself had been respected and wealthy London merchants before the 1700s. David's father Jacob had emigrated to New York where he pursued the family business and many cultural interests, and where David was born. Jacob was the Crown's agent for North America. Nevertheless, numerous members of the family remained in London, and indeed two of David's brothers returned there to serve in the family's mercantile interests and became extremely wealthy and successful.[6] The London ties were most helpful. Under the circumstances there was more than the usual amount of correspondence in the Franks family, and numerous letters have survived from this early period.

With this strong background of family support David arrived in Philadelphia in 1740 to engage in business, also as a merchant. He was but twenty years of age, but he and his slightly older brother Moses at once formed a partnership which imported all kinds of dry goods and hardware. Soon, however, Moses left for England to join in business with their older brother, and David in turn formed a new partnership with his uncle Nathan Levy.[7] This was a period of strong growth for Philadelphia which, in addition to its own increasing needs, was the gateway to and the supplier of goods for the whole of the province of Pennsylvania. The firm's interests expanded rapidly to include the chartering and ownership of ships carrying exports from the colonies to London and returning with manufactured and other dry goods which could be bought at

David Franks and his sister Phila
painted in New York by an unknown artist

American Jewish Historical Society

their warehouse. One of their ships, the *Myrtilla,* arrived in Philadelphia in the late summer of 1752, probably carrying the famous Liberty Bell which was ordered to commemorate the fiftieth anniversary of William Penn's Charter of Liberties for Pennsylvania.[8] It was prophetically inscribed "Proclaim Liberty throughout all the land to all the inhabitants thereof," cracked, but promptly recast. David Franks' career was to run afoul of those words.

By 1743 Franks was in a position to marry. Margaret Evans, daughter of Philadelphia's Register of Wills, became his bride just before Christmas. Margaret had close connections with the Pennsylvania proprietors. In 1704 her father, Peter Evans, had accompanied his cousin to Philadelphia when the latter became Lieutenant Governor of Pennsylvania upon appointment by William Penn. Peter had studied law at London's Middle Temple and at the time of her marriage to Franks[9] had been the Register for Philadelphia County for many years.

A good indication of the Franks family's wealth and position is found in portions of a silver tea service at the Metropolitan Museum of Art. These are most handsome and beautifully decorated pieces made by Paul de Lamerie, the famous Huguenot silversmith of eighteenth century London: a tea kettle and stand, a bread or cake basket and a waste bowl, all bearing the coat-of-arms of the Franks impaling those of the Evans family. No Franks except David married an Evans. They bear Lamerie's hallmarks identifying their manufacture in 1744-1745. There seems no doubt that the tea service was ordered by one of the Franks family residing in or near London (probably David's brother Naphtali) when word was received of David's approaching marriage, was completed the following year, and was forwarded from London as a wedding present (although the armorial engraving was probably added in the 1750s). The work was done during Lamerie's later years when the rococo style, with much ornament, was in fashion.[10]

Even before his own marriage, David became allied with another New York family destined because of its wealth and position to become Tories thirty years later. In September, 1742 his sister Phila eloped in New York with Oliver De Lancey. As David reported it in a letter in the Spring of 1743, "all the family in N York were well last fryday . . . but in very great uneasiness & great Concern on Acc[oun]t of Philla's being Marry'd to Oliver D

The Metropolitan Museum of Art, New York

David and Margaret Franks' Tea Kettle and Stand by Lamerie, ca. 1744

Lancy, she has been Marriy'd in Sep[tembe]r Last ye 8th & not a Soul Knew of it till Last week when she absented herself & went to his Country house where she has Remain'd Since & not been in town. I was very much Surpris'd when I heard it . . . am told he [father] is and my Mother in great grief about [it]."[11] Despite his parents' regret at marriage into a Church of England family,[12] the alliance stood David in good stead until the years of the Revolution. At that time his brother-in-law raised a regiment in New York supporting the British cause and was appointed a Brigadier General in the British Army with the expectation that he would recruit great numbers of Loyalists. He became the senior Loyalist officer in the British Army in America. He had inherited a splendid house at Broad and Pearl Streets, New York, where, during its later years as the city's most genteel place of public entertainment, many patriot meetings took place. In its Long Room Washington bade farewell at the end of the Revolution to his officers, more than forty of our greatest military leaders, with a celebrated address delivered in a highly emotional meeting. The mansion still stands, known as Fraunce's Tavern, and is open to the public.[13]

The decade of the 1750s saw very considerable business expansion for Franks. By 1751 the firm's store on Front Street was replaced as headquarters by the largest house on Second Street, near Walnut, later known as the Slate Roof House. Substantial western trade was developing. To improve its position in this, the firm established representation in Lancaster, about sixty miles to the west of Philadelphia. Even the heavy losses suffered in the French and Indian Wars proved to be not more than a temporary setback.[14]

Because of the risks to merchandise travelling to and from the west, Franks readily supported his partner Levy's enthusiasm for a Pennsylvania militia for military defense against the Indians and the French—a subject raised by several of the provincial governors with the Assembly. When in 1755 Governor Morris asked it to ordain a militia, it responded only by granting money "to the king's use" under a requirement that the Penn estates be proportionately taxed to raise the specified amount. The governor protested that he had no authority to assent on those terms. Franks was one of twenty public-spirited citizens who moved at once to heal the breach by subscribing to pay the five thousand pounds estimated as the Penn family's tax.[15]

It was at the time of the French and Indian Wars that, through family connections in London, David Franks and his father in New York entered upon a relationship which ultimately led to David's losing not only Woodford Mansion, but his wealth and his very considerable standing attained in the colonies. They became the official agents and contractors for the British army in North America. Nearly three years after Braddock's defeat young George Washington, then a Colonel in the British Army, wrote to Franks May 1, 1758 ordering supplies for his troops and equipment for himself. Franks replied by letter to Washington dated June 27. He had the satisfaction of learning that Fort Pitt was taken in November with Washington's assistance. Franks and his associates handled more than seven hundred and fifty thousand pounds of provisioning contracts during the wars.[16]

Now Franks' activities spread to other enterprises, including marine insurance and even soap manufacturing and candle making. He was, as well, involved in trading with friendly Indians. In 1759 Richard Peters, agent for the Penn interests, wrote to the Governor General of the Province asking that Franks be paid for silver "truck" he had secured for the use of the Indians expected to sign a treaty at Easter. In the Spring of 1761 Franks was billed for the purchase of stocks of Indian "heart broaches" from the Philadelphia silversmith, Joseph Richardson. At the end of 1762 he was still active in this field, supplying silver "moon and half-moon gorgets."[17]

In the 1760's tensions were beginning to build with England, which needed money to defend its colonies. Franks saw matters in the same light as many other local merchants when he signed Philadelphia's Non-Importation Agreement late in 1765,[18] helping to secure repeal of the Stamp Act.

The aftermath of the French and Indian Wars brought Franks, along with many others, into a frenzied acquisition of interests in western lands. By the Peace Treaty of 1763 the French were deprived of any interest in the area between Pittsburgh and the Illinois territory. A new surge westward, although it encountered new losses because of continuing Indian attacks, led Franks to acquire interests in land in Indiana in the mid-1760s, as well as in Illinois, Virginia and Pennsylvania.[19] Years passed, but the western land ownerships did not increase in value because expansion into the areas by settlers was slowed by Indian troubles and the approach of the Revolution.

An event early in 1768 further contributed to Franks' naturally royalist leanings. In January his oldest child, Abigail, married Andrew Hamilton, whose brother William owned The Woodlands, one of the finest country homes in the surroundings of Philadelphia—still standing in Woodlands Cemetery and looking directly down a long stretch of the Schuylkill. Andrew was the grandson of the lawyer and multiple officeholder in Pennsylvania of the same name, whose successful defense of Peter Zenger gave rise to the term "Philadelphia lawyer," as well as the nephew of a governor of the colony—and thus again one of the close-knit group of the provincial hierarchy acting under Penn's descendants in England. Andrew's brother "Billy" was to be linked with Franks as an alleged Tory lawbreaker during the Revolution.[20]

Another handsome piece of David and Margaret Franks' silver, now in the possession of the Historical Society of Pennsylvania, bears the date of Abigail's wedding day, January 6, 1768. Inscribed with their names, it is a salver by the American maker, Myer Myers. In the following December they celebrated their own twenty-fifth anniversary.

The Historical Society of Pennsylvania

Salver by Myer Myers monogrammed D M F, ca. 1768

David's purchase of Woodford in 1771 linked the mansion with two other great American houses, The Woodlands in Philadelphia and Fraunces' Tavern in New York—all three of which survive today. He promptly made additions to Woodford for the comfort of his wife and children. On March 14, 1772 he and Margaret borrowed four hundred pounds from the Coleman executors and gave a mortgage on the mansion later satisfied without having been recorded.[21] By the Fall of that year the work was complete, and in November Franks secured a new insurance survey. It described the house as being two stories high and as containing the handsome stairwell and Palladian window so admired today, as well as a new kitchen wing surmounted by a large panelled room which could have been a ballroom.[22] With very substantial family connections in England and New York and ties by marriage with certain wealthy and influential families, and with large interests in property to protect, including Woodford, David and Margaret had a natural sympathy with the Loyalists which would carry over when war came.

Yet the Franks were not immune to tragedy. On August 24, 1774 the *Pennsylvania Gazette* reported:

> On Sunday evening last, after five days illness, died, in her prime of life, Miss Polly Franks, second daughter of David Franks, Esq; of this city—a young lady whose sweetness of temper, elegance of manners, cheerful conversation and unblemished virtue, endeared her to all her connexions, and especially to her now mournful parents, who found her in every part of life a shining example of filial duty and affection. Her remains were interred, on Monday forenoon, in Christ-Church burying ground, amid the tears of her numerous acquaintance and relatives.

It has been estimated from a study of the tax lists of that year that ten percent of the city's population owned nearly ninety percent of its taxable property.[23] The Franks were duly listed. David retained the two blacks for whom he had been taxed in 1769. In the intervening years he had added a horse to make four, and two cows to make three.[24] The horses were probably quartered both in town and at Woodford plantation, which was listed as the Franks "country seat." Commuting the four miles from the city to Woodford along the Wissahickon Road in comfort required one's own carriage. In 1772 the Franks were listed as one of only eighty-four carriage owners in a city of some twenty thousand

Philadelphians, a clear indication of the aristocratic and prestigious group in which they moved. They had in fact appeared in an earlier carriage census of 1761 as one of only twenty-nine families owning carriages, when they were listed as having two.[25]

Yet David Franks did not own his town house. Renting rather than owning one's house in the city was common practice in the eighteenth century, when probably not more than one fifth of all Philadelphians owned their own homes.[26] One of the grandest of the houses was that built by William Logan in the 1750s. The son of William Penn's confidential secretary who was also Chief Justice of Pennsylvania and at one time President of the Privy Council and ex officio Governor of the Province, Logan himself was active in provincial governmental affairs as a member of the Council. He died in October, 1776, having until then maintained both his inherited country home of Stenton and the town house he had built on South Second Street north of Walnut in the heart of the small area of closely-knit families. Apparently late in 1776, David Franks rented the Logan city mansion—a splendid large three-story brick house of double width and stately proportions containing twelve rooms in addition to the kitchen and garret and having its own garden, stable and coach house.[27] His choice must have been due not only to its character but also to the fact that it sat just across the street from the Slate Roof House, his place of business. By the end of the year Logan's daughter, Sarah Logan Fisher, was receiving friendly visits from Franks in town such as one on December 26 when she noted in her diary that "David Franks came yesterday from New York & brought a York newspaper which we looked upon as a great prize."[28]

The clouds of approaching conflict with the mother country had begun to burst in 1774. Boston was occupied and the First Continental Congress assembled in Philadelphia for concerted action. Woodford must have become an ever greater haven from town concerns. In the early phases of the War, before the British took Philadelphia and hard lines of division were established, it was possible for the Franks to use their country home as much as they desired. But it too was to be caught up in the struggle of the Revolution.

The Franks' youngest child Rebecca was now blooming into one of the outstanding belles of Philadelphia. She was known for her quick wit and turn of phrase as well as for beauty. But it was only with the British occupation of the city in the Fall of 1777 that Rebecca's obvious preference for the British officers, and the close relationship of her set with them, swung the public image of the Franks family far more to the Tory side than David ever expected. Although his wife undoubtedly had a quite conservative outlook, it seems to have been Rebecca who pulled ahead and crystalized her mother's attitude.

Yet for his part personally, David was still trusted in the early period of hostilities as simply a responsible businessman. He was appointed at Congress' request to provide for the British prisoners held in the rebel stockades in Lancaster, Reading and Easton. Early in 1776 Washington suggested in a letter to John Hancock, President of the Congress, that if Franks would appoint a deputy to provide for the prisoners in Massachusetts, "It will save me much time and much trouble." Then in June, 1777 Franks became an assistant to Elias Boudinot, who was appointed American Commissary-General of prisoners, responsible for the welfare of both British and Americans.[29]

Had this been all, Franks might never have been caught up in the tightening web of circumstance. But through his brother Moses in London he had also been named agent for supplying the British troops, and after this, General Howe had appointed him to supply the English who were held prisoners by the Americans.[30] Congress accepted this duality. Yet Franks was now faced with peremptory orders from the British side of the conflict which in the light of his contract he dare not ignore. One issued from Boston in February, 1776:

> I have it in command from His Excellency The Honorable William Howe Commander in Chief of His Majesty's forces; that you continue to Victual his Majesty's 7th and 26th Regiments, the Royal Artillery, Scotch Emigrants and others of his Majesty's Troops who may be prisoners within the Limits of your Contract, at the usual Allowance.

Washington himself received this letter and forwarded it to the President of Congress with the request that its instructions be carried out. Another order sent from New York in February, 1777 is extant:

> It is the General's wish that you continue to victual such of His Majesty's Troops as are prisoners with you either in your Province the Jersies or Maryland if possible, also the Cana-

dians wheresoever they may be confined . . . with respect to the back Rations these Gentlemen claim, I cannot see the propriety of paying them for them, if they have been victuald by the Americans, it will be charged to Government as we bring a charge against the Americans for Victualling their Prisoners.[31]

While at first the British paid Franks promptly, he later encountered increasing difficulty in being paid at all for the goods and services he supplied. At the same time the American Congress, which at first had permitted payment by the British to be made in bills of credit, later required payment in specie in its effort to maintain the stability of the Continental currency. Franks' agents needed similar payments to replenish their funds advanced for Franks' account. They threatened to discontinue their services unless so paid. But specie was daily becoming rarer. By October, 1776 Franks' finances were suffering because of Britain's tardiness in repaying him for his outlays, to the extent that he requested permission to visit New York with his clerk in order to negotiate his claims personally. The trip was permitted on condition that they "give their parole not to give any intelligence to the enemy, and that they will return to this city"—but it failed to solve the problem.[32]

When, after the battle of the Brandywine in the Fall of 1777 the British entered Philadelphia without a battle, Franks stayed on as did most of the merchants, still hoping that he could present an image of neutrality to the Patriots. At about the time when the fall of Fort Mifflin opened the Delaware to British supplies, he was among many citizens signing an agreement to accept the colonial paper currency in lieu of gold and silver.[33]

It was now that any effort at evenhandedness in dealing with the two warring sides was in great measure taken out of her father's hands by Rebecca. She consorted openly and engagingly with Howe's officers, and indeed with General Howe himself. In February, 1778 she wrote to Nancy Paca, her close friend in Maryland:

> I spent Tuesday evening at Sir Wm. Howes where we had a concert and Dance . . . No loss for partners, even I am engaged to seven different gentlemen for you must know 'tis a fix'd rule never to dance but two dances at a time with the same person . . . I know you are as fond of a gay life as

myself—you'd have an opportunity of rakeing as much as you choose either at Plays, Balls Concerts or Assemblys. I've been but 3 evenings alone since we mov'd to town. I begin now to be almost tired.[34]

Rebecca would be twenty in another month.

Franks' town house was near that which General Howe first occupied—the Cadwalader house, one of the city's finest, on Second Street below Spruce. According to John McAllister, Jr., who in the 1850s was extremely well versed in the lore of the city, an old lady who during the British occupation lived nearly opposite the Franks related to McAllister that Rebecca was "a remarkably sprightly girl" with whom Howe relieved the rigors of his daytime duties. "He spent most of his time at Franks' house, enjoying the society of the chatty Miss Franks—they would chase each other from the house to the street and then back again." The old lady reported that "Howe was fat and waddling, and Miss Franks could soon chase him out of breath." According to McAllister, his informant used to raise her hands at the end of her narrative, exclaiming—"Such carryings on as there were between them!"[35] This was one of Howe's innocent diversions with an aristocratic youngster enamoured of the British uniform while he was living with his mistress, Mrs. Loring.

Woodford probably played a part in the social triumph of the Franks family during the short period until May, 1778, when Howe was called home to defend his inaction and the British command thought it best to consolidate its position in New York. But the area was not really secure. The British held Germantown, yet the land between it and the city was subject to scattered raids, particularly by brave patriot officers like Captain Allen McLane, a native Philadelphian who commanded certain American outposts that he covered on horse.[36] But despite Rebecca's participation in the balls, teas and amateur theatricals of the occupied city, the fact that Franks was still active in assisting both sides of the conflict may have kept the persons of his family and his country seat safe from molestation. Rebecca wrote letters from Woodford at this period.

Whatever feeling of security there was in this dual position was ended by Rebecca's prominent participation in the British farewell ball to General Howe, planned and staged by Major John André and Rebecca's first cousin Oliver De Lancey, Jr., in May, 1778. An occupant by forceful takeover of Franklin's house, André was a

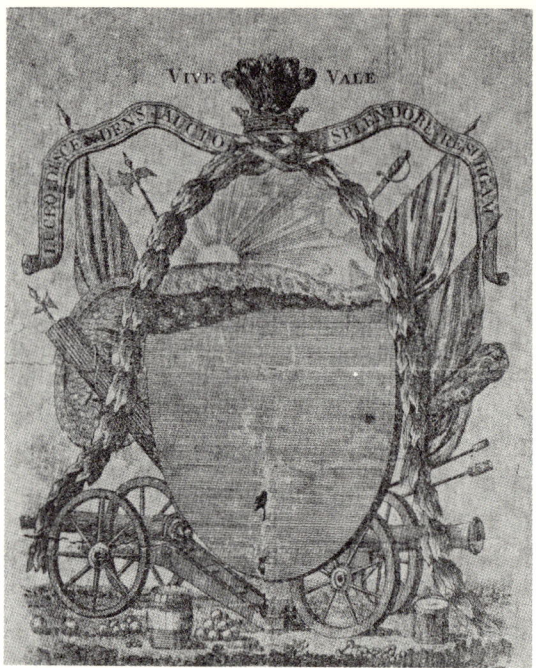

Library Company of Philadelphia

Ticket for the Mischianza Ball

talented amateur artist who is said to have been a frequent visitor at the Franks and to have occupied himself there as early as 1775 by painting a miniature of Rebecca.[37] What more natural than that Rebecca should be one of the small group of honored young ladies at the famed Mischianza Ball, for whose favor the medieval pageantry of jousting was revived by British officers caparisoned as knights? There was, too, her well-known beauty. Even the serious and recently-married Robert Barclay of London, having seen Rebecca on his trip to America in 1773, had singled her out in his thoughts when writing to America four years later: "What is become of Becky—is she yet settled?"[38]

A procession of ornamental barges floated the guests and the British officers a mile down the Delaware from the wharfs of Philadelphia to the field where ceremonies began in the late afternoon at Walnut Grove, the commandeered estate of deceased Quaker Joseph Wharton. The jousting was followed by a lavish banquet in a hall of mirrors created by André. Some seven hundred and fifty engraved tickets were issued to the chosen civilian population, and three hundred and thirty covers laid. Dancing until dawn brought to its highest achievement the kind of British activities which captured Becky's mind.[39] Fires and explosions during the ball caused by American forces under Captain McLane outside the city[40] did nothing to dispel her illusion of British scarlet and gold armed might.

But the Americans attacked not only by arms. They used the pen as well. The perhaps innocent female Philadelphians who dared to participate in this final display while the rebel troops were slowly reforming after a near-disastrous winter at Valley Forge, were castigated in a public letter soon sent by no less a personage than General Anthony Wayne:

> Tell those Philadelphia ladies, who attended Howe's assemblies and levees that the heavenly, sweet, pretty red coats—and the accomplished gentlemen of the guards and grenadiers—have been humbled on the plains of Monmouth. The Knights of the Blended Rose and of the Burning Mount have resigned their laurels to Rebel officers, who will lay them at the feet of those virtuous daughters of America who cheerfully gave up ease and affluence in a city, for liberty and peace of mind in a cottage.[41]

In little more than an hour after the British released their hold on the city, the tattered Americans marched into it to observe the British withdrawal by boat for their march across New Jersey. It was an extremely tense moment for their sympathizers.

Upon the withdrawal of the British troops, Rebecca's mother may well have removed her from the alarums of the city. With the return of the Patriots active animosity against the Tories reached riotous proportions and made their position very uncomfortable. Yet Rebecca appears soon to have attended another ball, perhaps one given by the Whigs in honor of the newly-arrived French officers.[42] Some of the Tory ladies were invited, none the less, to make an agreeable company.[43] David Franks' dual position may have brought an invitation to Rebecca. It was probably such a later ball, rather than the Mischianza about which she wrote:

> When I think of it. oh! The Ball—not a lady there—the Committee of *real* Whigs met in the Afternoon & frightened the Beaux so much that they went round to all the ladies *that meant* to go to desire they'd stay at Home. Tho it seems the Committee had no thoughts of molesting [us] being all of their

own Kidney. I'm delighted that it came to nothing, as they had the impudence to laugh at US . . . when the roads will permit my return God knows.[44]

Franks had no way of knowing it, but he had only the coming summer of 1778 and two others to enjoy such use as he could make of the country seat he had so carefully enlarged. The physical fortifications the British had erected between the city and Woodford were dismantled;[45] but though Franks was theoretically free to come and go, he was automatically placed under suspicion by the returning patriots; and as the first step in his downfall, his own rashness quickly put him in prison.

With his usual attitude that business came first, he was forced to continue communications with the British in New York to collect their debt owing him for his provisioning of their prisoners. In October, 1778 he failed to confine two letters to business subjects. In one, written to Captain Thomas Moore, of his brother-in-law De Lancey's regiment in New York, Franks reported that at the preceding midnight "Billy Hamilton," his daughter Abigail's brother-in-law, had been honorably acquitted of treason by a jury after only a couple of minutes' deliberation.[46] This was not damning in itself, but in the letter to Moore, Franks enclosed a separate one to Franks' brother Moses in London. After covering business details, he reported again on Hamilton's acquittal and this time referred to his being for twelve hours "a prisoner at the bar." "People are taken and confined at the pleasure of every scoundrel. Oh what a situation Britain has left its friends . . ."

The two letters were intercepted. Only three days after they were written the Continental Congress considered their contents and resolved:

> That the contents of the said letter manifest a disposition and intentions inimical to the safety and liberties of the United States; and that Mr. Franks, having endeavoured to transmit this letter by stealth within the British lines, has abused the confidence reposed in him by Congress, to exercise within the jurisdiction of these states the office of commissary to the British prisoners.
> Resolved, That General Arnold be directed to cause the said David Franks forthwith to be arrested, and conveyed to the new gaol in this city, there to be confined till the further order of Congress.

Resolved, That David Franks, Esq. be not, after the 10th day of November next, permitted to exercise, directly or indirectly, the office of commissary to the British prisoners within the jurisdiction of the United States.

Resolved, That General Washington be directed to transmit a copy of these resolutions to Sir Henry Clinton, and to inform him, that Congress desire he will nominate a proper person who, having received their approbation, may exercise the office of commissary to the British prisoners.

Ordered, That the committee [to which Franks' letter was referred] sit again, and consider by what process it may be proper to take cognizance of Mr. D. Franks's offence.[47]

It is ironical from today's viewpoint that Benedict Arnold, who later became America's most infamous traitor, apprehended and imprisoned David Franks who was never proven to be one at all. But so it was, and Franks replaced one of the American Patriot prisoners who in great numbers had been among the very first to be confined in their own new jail on Walnut Street at Sixth. His stay of perhaps two weeks ended after he wrote two letters which were read on the floor of the Congress.[48]

Release from prison did not mean the end of Franks' deep troubles, either businesswise or personally. He continued his efforts to obtain payment from the British and at the end of January, 1779, less than three months after his release, he petitioned the Supreme Executive Council of Pennsylvania that his clerk, Patrick Rice, be given a pass to New York to settle Franks' accounts. This was a hot potato which the Council was loath to take a position upon and referred to Congress itself. A few days later, with its approval, the Council granted the pass as a "Special Case."[49] But the trip must have been unsuccessful.

In another ninety days Franks came to trial before the Pennsylvania Supreme Court on the charge of a misdemeanor in giving intelligence to the enemy. The *Pennsylvania Packet* reported that after the trial began on a Saturday, the jury deliberated until 8 o'clock Sunday morning, when he was found not guilty. With this action the newspaper violently disagreed. It printed his two letters in full, attacked him, and forcibly stated that he should have been convicted.

Surely after this Franks should have been exceedingly circumspect and abandoned all direct communications with the British. Two circumstances may have contributed to his misreading the temper of the Americans about his case. One was that the Patriot General Charles Lee, retiring to Philadelphia after the battle of Monmouth, struck up a friendship of sorts with the irrepressible Rebecca, aspects of which were reported in the public press. Another lay in the efforts of an unidentified friend of Franks to come to his aid by a letter to the same newspaper which had attacked him. To this defender the effort to malign Franks and his jurors "must excite the indignation of every friend to his country, every friend to trial by Jury, and every lover of good order in society."[50]

In his continued efforts to recover financially, Franks attempted to liquidate the investments he had made in western lands. Two of the land companies were combined in June, 1779 under his presidency. This did not produce the cash he so needed; but he was trying every avenue to avoid financial disaster and hold onto what property was left at home, including Woodford. There was no alternative to still further efforts at payment from the British. He set about this by again petitioning the Council in December for permission to go to New York personally. He was sent for and examined by the Council, but now he was alleged by an informer to be involved in smuggling British imports into Philadelphia and was met with a rejection.[51]

When, in late September, 1780, Arnold surrendered West Point and André was hanged, Franks came to the end of the road. The Patriots simply had to clean house. Everything collapsed at once. Three days after the defection his beloved wife Margaret died. Only four days later the Council resolved that both Franks and William Hamilton be arrested as "persons whom there is just reason to suspect are enemies to the American cause, and to hold an unlawfull and dangerous correspondence and intercourse with the enemy at New York." Franks was again committed to jail and within a few days was ordered to depart with Hamilton within fourteen days for the enemy lines "and not return again to any of these United States during the continuance of the present war," each giving security of two hundred thousand pounds. After an unsuccessful petition for delay, Franks responded October 13 by again petitioning the Council:

> That being order'd by your honorable Board to depart from this State, and go within the Enemies' Lines, he finds it necessary to remove his Family with him. He therefore prays

your Honours to grant a Pass for his Daughter, two Maid Servants, one Man Servant, and their baggage.[52]

No wonder Franks became ill. His second petition for an extension of time, now grounded on "indisposition of body," was answered by sending a physician to examine him in prison.[53] This gained Franks an extra month to settle his affairs. On November 1 his library was sold at auction out of the house on Second Street. Its size required several sale sessions and may well have been swelled by volumes brought to town from Woodford. Its length also demonstrated that Franks was, indeed, interested in more than mercantile pursuits. Among the volumes then dispersed, bearing his signature, and which remain extant were "The Annals of Europe" for the year 1739 in two volumes and for 1740, and a series of numerous volumes of the debates of Parliament in London.[54]

The pass to New York was issued on November 18 with the suggestion by the Council that on further disobedience to the mandate for banishment, compulsory measures would be adopted. Franks replied on November 20 asking to remain until the 23rd. This was granted, but President Reed informed him that he was now expected to set out for New York and that in the opinion of the Council his excuses were frivolous and would warrant no further indulgences.[55]

There was nothing for it but to obey, and Franks did so, even as he was still settling his affairs. There was no order confiscating any of his property, and one of his last acts was to sign on the 22nd a deed prepared by the scrivener to transfer Woodford to Thomas Paschall. Franks had been indebted to Paschall since 1775 and had given him a mortgage on Woodford.[56] Clearly Franks had hoped to pay his debt in full before leaving, for during the preceding month he had been able to discharge much of it. Now he transferred the property for a credit of thirteen hundred thirty pounds against the remainder, leaving only a small balance due but leaving Woodford still subject to the original first mortgage given by Alexander and Rebecca Barclay in 1769 to the Coleman estate for five hundred pounds.

With Franks and Rebecca in New York, where he had assumed his payment problems could readily be resolved, he now found contrariwise that a good part of his attention had to remain in Philadelphia. He had left his records there with his agents. On the very day before he left he had written about the receipt of payment for many articles which he had placed on consignment.⁵⁷ In February, 1781 he received permission to return to Pennsylvania for four weeks to transact private business.⁵⁸ Writing from New York in May, 1782 to his Philadelphia agents, he referred to a number of properties he still owned in Philadelphia and to their possible sale for his benefit, "I being on the go to London in 2 or 3 days" to present his accounts.⁵⁹ It seems clear that with Rebecca's marriage in January of that year to a British Lieutenant Colonel, all three were moving to England, which he had always wanted to see. A few months later he wrote to Philadelphia from the estate inherited by his son Jacob's wife at Isleworth outside London, detailing his investments and tangled affairs including other transactions with Thomas Paschall "opposite the Church," requesting the forwarding of a protested bill of exchange remaining in his "Black Walnut Chest," and referring to matters reflected in his "Small Memorandum Book" he had left behind.⁶⁰

It was most difficult to turn lands and mortgages into cash. Payment from the British did not materialize. In January, 1783 he wrote of his intention to return to America "when times are settled," and in April of that year he received a passport to travel to New York;⁶¹ but no record has been found showing that he made the trip. The inference is otherwise, for he was almost destitute and shortly afterwards referred again to returning at a later date: in a letter sent from Isleworth in July to his agent in Lancaster he wrote, "I am penniless as a beggar, and often [have] empty pockets. No person wants more than I doo, it would be Charity to help me, and [I] would be glad to Sell some Lands to Raise Money . . . when times are Settled and I may remain in Quietness, I shall return . . ."⁶² In 1786 he was harassed in England for debts and had to appoint his agents in Philadelphia, by a document recorded there, to liquidate for his creditors' benefit all his real estate and personal property in North America.⁶³

Despite the bleakness of his last years, Franks had had more of "that sprightly genius" in him than his mother had thought. He had been not only assiduous and honest in his trading efforts, but innovative. He had dared much, gained much, and lost much. His business career may be typified by the incident an American patriot a generation younger than Franks recounted in his reminiscences concerning Franks' building and fitting out two vessels at Kensington, then just north of Philadelphia and now a part of it. These were most unusual since they were built entirely of logs and planks, apparently lashed together for the purpose of both carrying and serving as bulk cargo. One of them broke up at sea, while the other arrived safely in England with its burden.[64] And Franks had certainly transmitted a large ingredient of that sprightly genius to his daughter Rebecca's makeup!

It was surely still another effort to recover his former wealth which brought him back to Philadelphia in 1789 when he had "the gout in my hand"[65] and wrote with difficulty, as well as in 1791[66] and 1792.[67] He had been born in America and had spent the fruitful portion of his adult life in Philadelphia. The David Franks, merchant, who died there in the yellow fever epidemic of 1793[68] can hardly be other than he.[69] His will of 1785 was proved in London on July 22, 1794.[70] In it he expressed confidence that his lands in Pennsylvania, Virginia, Indiana and Illinois were worth more than his debts and left his property to his four children, with preference to Jacob "for his and his wife's very kind attention to me." His two sons in England were appointed to carry out the will along with his agent Tench Coxe of Philadelphia.

Mercantile reputations are difficult to sustain down through the years and Franks' case is no exception. But his name remains indelibly connected with the heyday of Woodford and has been preserved in the annals of the development of western Pennsylvania: for him Frankstown, Pennsylvania was named.

Rebecca Franks,
Tory Belle

For Rebecca Franks, just out of her teens, the world changed radically with the departure of the British from Philadelphia in June, 1778 and the return of the Patriots. Their attitude toward families of known Tory sympathies who had remained in the city during its occupation can readily be imagined. They were in no mood to reflect that it was only natural for people of wealth and prestige under the old order, and especially those who had enjoyed directly favors bestowed by the Crown, to be satisfied with life as it was and even to have taken all its benefits. Although Rebecca had seen little except the glitter of the surface she, like all the local Tories, was disappointed and dismayed when her champions voluntarily left her family to what the incoming American administration under Benedict Arnold might allot. With the disappointment, the gay life of entertainment she had known fell away. In her words:

> News you ask for, alas where is there any that *we* call good. For my part I have given up the thoughts of hearing any more. What's become of all the Beaux. I'm afraid they've quite deserted this road.

"This road" was the Wissahickon Road and Rebecca's letter to Betsy Shippen in the city was written from Woodford, for in it she also said "I would have sent the carriage over for you & your sisters this Afternoon but John has taken the Horses to Town to be shod."[1]

The atmosphere of Loyalist Philadelphia during the occupation as one of wanton luxury stood in stark contrast to this. As soon as the royal Army had settled down, the officers had formed eating clubs to occupy the time. There were the Yorkshire Club, the Friendly Brothers, the Loyal Association Club, and the "Society of Journeymen Tailors, modeled on the same plan as near as may be as those of London and Dublin." Balls were held weekly in the public rooms of the City Tavern, called simply "Smith's,"[2] which stood close below the Franks town house on Second Street above Walnut. It was a new building, the largest and most elegant public house in the colonies, yet it was modernized for the officers and their local consorts.[3] John Adams called Smith's "the most genteel in America."[4] The old South Street Theatre was reopened and produced a new play each week, given by a military theatrical troupe. General Howe entertained, proudly displaying his blonde mistress Mrs. Joshua Loring, whose husband was placated by an official appointment from Howe.[5] Prices rose until they were double in paper currency those quoted in hard money. The Quaker neutrals looked on, some content to take British gold and others highly critical. The young Tory girls of well-placed families (Rebecca was related by her sister's marriage to the Penns and the Allens)[6] were caught up in the froth of it all. Rebecca was constantly sought after and saw only the fun. As she wrote to her great friend Nancy Paca in Maryland:

> You can have no idea of the life of continued amusement I live in. I can scarce have a moment to myself. I have stole this while everybody is retired to dress for dinner. I am but just come from under Mr. J. Black's hands and most elegantly am I dressed for a ball this evening at Smith's where we have one every Thursday. You would not know the Room 'tis so much improv'd . . . I must go finish dressing as I'm engaged out to Tea.

Nancy, née Anne Harrison, now of Annapolis, had grown up with Rebecca in Philadelphia. Nancy had moved away when she married William Paca, who was a delegate from Maryland to the Continental Congress, a signer of the Declaration of Independence, and later a Governor of Maryland. Rebecca recounted the billeting of a British officer in Nancy's family's former home:

> Tell Mrs. Harrison she has got a gentleman in her house, who promises me not to let a single thing in it be hurt and I'm sure he'll keep his word—the family she left in it still remain.

In her letter to Nancy, written after the Franks "mov'd to town" as she mentioned in it, from Woodford, Rebecca described the flighty and most expensive fashions adopted by the fashionable Tory belles in these months:

> The Dress is more ridiculous and pretty than anything that ever I saw—great quantity of different coloured feathers on the head at a time besides a thousand other things. The Hair dress'd very high in the shape, Miss Vining's was the night we returned from Smiths—the Hat we found in your Mother's Closet wou'd be of a proper size. I have an afternoon cap with one wing—tho' I assure you I go less in the fashion than most of the Ladies—no being dress'd without a hoop.

Rebecca's letter to Nancy could have been harmful to her husband's position when Rebecca wrote concerning an evening spent at General Howe's:

> I asked his leave to send you a Handkerchief to show the fashions. He very politely gave me permission to send anything you wanted, tho' I told him you were a Delegate's Lady ... I send some of the most fashionable Ribbon and Gauze...[7]

Upon being shown this letter and the gifts Becky had sent, Paca immediately wrote to the Governor assuring him that neither Paca nor his wife had initiated the correspondence or solicited the presents received with it. Paca went so far as to give the Governor permission to bring the matter before the governing Council if he should consider it sufficiently material.[8]

A Hessian officer summed up the gaiety by reporting that "Assemblies, concerts, comedies, clubs, and the like make us forget there is any war, save it is a capital joke." But beneath this layer of amenity and gracious entertainment lay stark realities unknown to Rebecca. Only four blocks from her town house frightful cruelties were practiced upon American prisoners in the city's just-completed New Prison by its keeper, the British Provost Marshal William Cunningham, who ended on the gallows in London.[9] Every day victims died and were dragged out for burial in the adjoining potter's field, now Washington Square. The Redcoat officers took such things lightly. If Becky attended the theatre on its opening night, she surely failed to understand the reference when a Prologue ascribed to Major André was read containing a gory double entendre:

> In lofty terms old, vaunting Sadlers Wells
> Of her tight ropes and ladder-dancing tells;
> But Cunningham in both excels.[10]

But Rebecca seemed always physically safe. Later, in New York, when she went out at night unchaperoned, she wrote that "we Philadelphians, knowing no harm, feared none."[11]

Perhaps naturally accompanying the indolence and the combination of military show and laxity, immorality was rife in the town. The Tory belles were protected to a degree, for they were thrown with the British at the officer level. True, they were directly exposed to Howe's distasteful personal example; but at the same time they were the beneficiaries of his announced policy that if a young lady became pregnant by one of his officers, that officer would be forced to marry her. All knew this was no idle gesture, for Howe had enforced it in New York when he required a friend of André, Major Lord Cathcart, to marry the daughter of a local Tory.[12] In any case, the belles were looking for good husbands and were not to be deluded into an easy relationship; and some of the officers, at least, were wary of becoming too involved.

Evidence of loose behavior was everywhere and furnished another deterrent to those of Rebecca's group who knew they were above that kind of conduct. In her case it was very close at hand, as she recounted in a letter to Nancy Shippen:

> The afternoon before last I was standing at the door looking out for B. Redman & some others I expected when Griffin, H. Low and Mr. Cary came up to me. after talking a few minutes with me they walk'd off. Theres a house next door but one that a Mrs. McKoy lives in, a Lady well known to the gentlemen and don't you think Grif & Low had the impudence to go in while I was looking right at them. Cary came back to me and said as he was a Married Man he could not take such a liberty but they [had] only gone in to look at a tube rose. I told him I really did not know who liv'd there and looked as foolish as he did—the Lady was out thank god so they were disappointed. I never was half so angry in my life. I never think of it but I feel my face glow with rage. Tell Molly I hope she'll never have any more to say to Grif as long as she lives for my part and I allways disliked him . . . .[13]

The theatre had its many female hangers-on ready for anything, often the wives of British enlisted men. According to the doorkeeper, they were "generally of no character." The streets were little different. At a public review, a Major's mistress "rode down the whole line in an open carriage, her horses, servants, and her own person embellished in the colors of her lover's regiment." Such examples drew forth even from the Tory side such sallies in verse as:

> Awake, arouse Sir Billy
>   There's forage in the plain
> Ah, leave your little filly
>   And open the campaign.
> Heed not a woman's prattle
>   Which tickles in the ear
> But give the word for battle
>   And grasp the warlike spear.[14]

But life was too pleasant—to the great dismay of families like the Franks when, in the following Spring, they were left behind in the backwash.

Nor would Rebecca have been aware in any sense of the desperate straits of the tattered Continentals only twenty-five miles away at Valley Forge under Washington—without shoes, uniforms, blankets or even adequate food or shelter, in the grip of an extreme winter, dying daily as in Philadelphia but this time from disease and malnutrition; yet sustained by the efforts of Von Steuben to form them into a disciplined army and raised to the heights by an event a month before the British Mischianza: their army passed in review and listened to a reading of the new Treaty of Alliance with France,[15] of which word had just arrived and which in fact lost the war for the still-dawdling enemy.

But despite the relaxation in British ranks, there was a serious group of Redcoat officers of whom Major Henry Johnson was one. He was quartered in the house of a leading Quaker, Edward Pennington, at the corner of Race and Crown streets on the northern border of town. This was the headquarters of the Twenty-eighth Infantry and the resort of a number of more senior British officers who had a high opinion of Washington. When the Mischianza was on everyone's lips, a young member of the family where Johnson was quartered asked an old artillery major what was the distinction between the Knights of the Mountain and those of the Rose. "The knights of the Burning Mountain are *tom*fools, and the knights of the Blended Rose are *damned* fools. I know of no other difference between them. What will Washington think of all this?"[16] Rebecca knew Johnson in Philadelphia and may have referred to him, without name, in a letter which commenced:

> Dear Nancy,—You may see the above is not my writing a very smart beau I assure you wrote it but not being acquainted with your disposition was afraid to go on.[17]

Her keen analysis of character made it not a matter of chance that later in New York she realized the qualities of Johnson as opposed to those of the usual cavorting Redcoat—and married him.

While Rebecca was removed from the uproar in town after the return of the American forces, her mood became temporarily less vivacious. She confided:

> I begin to grow Home sick 'tis very dull such Weather for I hant a soul to speak to except Aunt nor a Book to read. I'm determined to send to Imlay for one this Afternoon. I hant seen a Beau Since the day before yesterday—where can the Wretches keep.[18]

But many are the stories of Rebecca's rapier-quick comprehension and repartee during the period after the British departure. One tells how, shortly thereafter, she was called upon by her Patriot friend Colonel Jack Stewart of Maryland. He had exchanged his well-worn uniform of Valley Forge for a handsome scarlet suit. Referring to Rebecca as having been one of the ladies honored at the Mischianza, he said,"I have adopted your colors my princess, the better to secure a courteous reception. Deign to smile on a true knight." Rebecca's reply was immediate. Turning to her companions, she exclaimed, "How the ass glories in the lion's skin!"[19]

On this same occasion, Rebecca's group witnessed a commotion in the streets which led to her outwitting Stewart, who played again with the same weapons. A civilian returning to the city described it:

> Last Saturday, an imitation of the Mischienza . . . was humbly attempted. A noted strumpet was paraded through the streets with her head dressed in the modern British taste, to the no small amusement of a vast crowd... She acted her part well...

Another who witnessed this display by one with ragged skirts and bare feet was the Patriot General Richard Henry Lee, who reported that he saw a —

Woman of the Town with the Monstrous headdress of the Tory Ladies . . . Her head was elegantly and expensively dressed, I suppose about three feet high and of proportionable width, with a profusion of Curls, &c &c &c — the figure was droll and occasioned much mirth—it has loosened some heads already and probably will bring the rest within the bounds of reason.[20]

When this coarse charade outdoors passed by Rebecca and her comrades, they peered out. The unfortunate Colonel could say only that "the lady was equipped altogether in the English fashion." But Rebecca had already perceived the intent of the mockery and commented, "Not altogether, Colonel; for though the style of her head is British, her shoes and stockings are in the genuine Continental fashion."[21]

The *Pennsylvania Packet* regarded Rebecca as good copy whose verbal thrusts would sell newspapers and reprinted her sally of animals putting on the lion's skin. This provoked her to a chiding letter to the publisher, filled with subtle humor:

Mr. Printer. There are many persons so unhappy in their disposition that, like the *dog* in the manger, they can neither enjoy the innocent pleasures of life themselves, nor in others without grumbling and *growling* . . .; hence it is, we so frequently observe hints and anecdotes in your Paper respecting the Commanding Officer, Head-Quarters and Tory Ladies. This mode of attacking characters is really admirable, and equally as polite as carreying slander and defamation by significant nods, winks and shrugs. Poor beings indeed who plainly indicate to what *species of animals they belong* by the badness of their conduct. [22][italics added]

In this period, too, Rebecca gave rise to a mock controversy in the press by asserting that the eccentric General Charles Lee of the American forces, who regarded her as "a lady who has had every human and divine advantage," wore green breeches "patched" with leather. In reply, he sent a brash and somewhat salacious letter with which he forwarded the breeches to her as proof that they were, instead, in the best European style. His letter was printed in January, 1779 in the *United States Magazine* and promptly reprinted by other newspapers. The Tory *Royal Gazette* of New York published his letter together with two forgeries said to constitute Rebecca's response. But upon learning that Rebecca had been vexed by his behavior, Lee wrote a letter of apology which he sent for publication to the *Pennsylvania Gazette*.[23] He was truly charmed by Rebecca and seems to have genuinely regretted causing her any embarrassment.

On one occasion Rebecca's impishness led to a prank at a reception Martha Washington was giving to the French Minister. She tied a black-and-white cockade like those worn in honor of the French Alliance to her dog's neck and bribed a servant to loose it into the ballroom.[24]

It was in this period, surrounded by many of the chief personages among the patriots, that Rebecca was quite probably the author of an unsigned political satire attacking prominent American leaders of the Revolution, in the form of a poem of some fifteen hundred lines. This was strongly acid in content, well fitting with the incident at the Washingtons' reception, and assuredly a tour de force amply illustrative of the intellectual brilliance of its author. Numerous manuscript copies were distributed. Many years later Benson J. Lossing, the well-known author of the *Field Book of the American Revolution,* edited the *American Historical Record* in which he published the satire in three installments under the title "A Loyalist's Poem." He stated that it had been found in manuscript form among the papers of Peter Kemble, a Loyalist who had lived in New York and New Jersey during the Revolution, whose son sent it to Lossing—who concluded from internal evidence that it was written probably in Philadelphia in the early autumn of 1779 when the Loyalists "were hopeful and active." Publication of the first installment elicited a letter sent in September, 1873 to Mr. Lossing by Peter Kemble's grandson, Gouverneur Kemble of New York, saying, "I find in the *Record* a satirical poem, written by a Lady in Philadelphia, during the Revolutionary War, who I remember to have seen at my Grandfather's[25] about the beginning of this century, who afterwards married an English Officer. General Scott met her at Bath, in England, after the War of 1812 . . . . He said she expressed regret at having taken sides against America in the war of the Revolution . . . The copy you have was found among my grandfather's papers and is no doubt genuine."[26] But this is a glimpse into Rebecca's future.

When she accompanied her father in his exile to New York at the end of November, 1780, she was an intriguing young lady of twenty-two years. She must have felt deeply for his welfare, for she could have stayed behind with her older sister and her friends, and she soon terminated a visit in the country outside New York because "I cannot bear Papa's being so much alone."[27] They were now at the nerve center of the British war effort, the seat of the British Army staff under General Sir Henry Clinton. Members of both her father's family and that of her aunt Phila and her uncle Oliver De Lancey lived there. Again she moved in the circles of the most influential families and of the British officers.

Her nimble wit and tart tongue did not leave her. At a ball given by the British, General Clinton, engaged in conversation with Rebecca, broke off to call to the musicians, "Give us *Britains, Strike Home.*" Rebecca at once exclaimed, "The Commander-in-Chief has made a mistake; he meant to say "Britains, *go* home." It has been said that she spared neither friend nor foe.[28]

Although this quick sally was at the expense of the British, Rebecca remained totally Loyalist in her outlook. In the summer of 1781 she left the city to visit at Flatbush,[29] where on August 10 she wrote to her sister Abigail in Philadelphia. She was maturing quickly. After many chatty subjects, she addressed herself seriously to the news received from her older brother in London of his intention to join the British Army:

> And now my dear Abby I am going to tell you a piece of news that you'll dislike as much as I do. What think you of Moses coming out with a cockade! He writes to Papa and me 'tis his serious resolve, and we must not be surprised if we see him this Summer. The idea of entering an Ensign at his time of life distresses [me] more than anything I've met with since I left you. All the comfort I have is that his uncle M. will not allow him. I have not had an opportunity of asking Papa's opinion of it, as I received the letters since I've been here; but I am certain he must disapprove of it as much as I do. Was he ten or twelve years younger I should not have the smallest objection,—but 'tis too late for him to enter into such a life,—and after the indulgence he's ever been used to he'll never brook being commanded from post to pillar by every brat of boy who may chance to be longer in the service. Tomorrow I shall write to him and make use of every argument I am mistress of to dissuade him from so mad a project, which I hope will arrive in time to prevent it, for if he once enters I would be the first to oppose his quitting it—as I ever lov'd a steady character. The danger of the war I have in a measure reconciled myself to. 'Tis only his age I object to and the dis-agreeable idea of his being sent the Lord knows where. If he does enter, which I hope to God he may not, I wish he may join the 17th, or else get into the Dragoons—the latter I think he'll prefer on account of his lameness.[30]

It was the 17th Infantry which was commanded by Lieutenant Colonel Henry Johnson, her friend from Philadelphia days.[31]

Rebecca's powers of observation and perceptiveness—a combination which entitled her to pre-eminence along with her beauty—are well shown in her acute comments on New York women. Her neighbors were the Van Horns:

> You ask a description of the Miss V[an] Horn that was with me—Cornelia—she is in disposition as fine a girl as ever you saw—a great deal of good humour and good sense. Her person is too large for a beauty, in my opinion, and yet I am not partial to a little woman; her complexion, eyes and teeth are very good, and a great quantity of light brown hair. (Entre nous, the girls of New York excell us Philadelphians in that particular and in their forms.) A sweet countenance and agreeable smile. Her feet, as you desire, I'll say nothing about—they are V[an] Horn's and what you'd call Willings. But her sister Kitty is the belle of the family I think, tho' some give the preference to Betsy. You'll ask how many thousand there are, only five. Kitty's form is much in the stile of our admir'd Mrs. Galloway, but rather taller and larger—her complexion very fine, and the finest hair I ever saw. Her teeth are beginning to decay, which is the case of most N[ew] Y[ork] girls after eighteen: and a great deal of elegance of manner. By the by, few New York ladies know how to entertain company in their own houses unless they introduce the card tables except this family, (who are remarkable for their good sense and ease). I don't know a woman or girl that can chat above half an hour, and that on the form of a cap, the colour of a ribbon or the set of a hoop-stay. I will do our ladies, that is Philadelphians, the justice to say they have more cleverness in the turn of an eye than the N[ew] Y[ork] girls have in their whole composition. With what ease, have I seen a Chew, a Penn, Oswald, Allen, and a thousand others entertain a large circle of both sexes, and the conversation without the aid of cards not flag or seem the least strain'd or stupid. Here, or more properly speaking in N[ew] Y[ork], you enter the room with a formal set curtsey and after the how do's, 'tis a fine, or a bad day, and those trifling nothings are finish'd, all's a dead calm 'till the cards are introduced, when you see pleasure dancing in the eyes of all the matrons and they seem to gain new life. The misses, if they have a favourite swain, frequently decline playing for the pleasure of making love—for to all appearances 'tis the ladies and not the gentlemen, that shew a preference nowadays. 'Tis here, I fancy, always leap year. For my part that am used to quite another mode of behaviour, I cannot help shewing my surprise, perhaps they call it ignorance, when I see a lady

> single out her pet to lean almost in his arms at an Assembly or playhouse, (which I give my honour I have too often seen both in married and single), and to hear a lady confess a partiality for a man who perhaps she has not seen three times. Well, I declare such a gentleman is a delightful creature, and I could love him for my husband,—or I could marry such or such a person; and scandal says most who have been married, the advances have first come from the ladie's side, or she has got a male friend to introduce him and puff her off. 'Tis really the case, and with me they lose half their charms,—and I fancy there wou'd be more marriage was another mode adopted; but they've made the men so saucy that I sincerely believe the lowest Ensign thinks 'tis but ask, and have,—a red coat and smart epaulette is sufficient to secure a female heart.

We have Rebecca's letter only because it never reached its destination but was intercepted and retained by the authorities.[32]

In New York her popularity with the male sex remained great. In the course of writing her letter from Flatbush to her sister she had to stop because "General Robertson, Commodore Affleck and Major Murray made their appearance," and moments later "Two more beaux,—Captain Affleck and a Mr. Biddulph—,the first frightful, the other very genteel and clever."

> Yesterday the Grenadiers had a race at the Flatlands, and in the afternoon this house swarm'd with beaux and some very smart ones. How the girls wou'd have envy'd me cou'd they have peep'd and seen how I was surrounded, and yet I shou'd have [felt] as happy if not much more to have spent the afternoon with the Thursday Party at the Woodlands.

On another subject, the letter referred to Abby's last to Rebecca:

> You beg to know what my presents are . . . . The shoes or rather patterns for them, are dark maroon and embroidered with gold, and the other, white with pink. She [Rebecca's Aunt Richa] says she hopes they'll be wedlock shoes—which I much doubt. The dear good old lady seems on the fidgets to have me married.

Despite the doubts Rebecca thus expressed in August, 1781, her relationship with Henry Johnson—probably in her mind when she mentioned her hope that her brother might join the 17th Foot he led—matured quickly after her return to New York City. On Monday, January 28, 1782 the *New York Gazette and Weekly Mercury* reported that "last Thursday evening was married at her father's house in Broadway, Miss Franks, youngest daughter of David Franks Esq. to Henry Johnson Esq., nephew to General Walsh and Lieut. Colonel to the XVII Regiment foot."[33]

Johnson was Rebecca's senior by ten years and had already seen much Army action. She had apparently known him a second time in Philadelphia when the British garrison was taken there from its capture at Stony Point in the summer of 1779.[34] He had been appointed an Ensign in the British Army at the age of only thirteen and by 1775 had come to America with the rank of Major under General Howe and participated in the Battle of Long Island. After the British left Philadelphia he was promoted and given command of the 17th Regiment of light infantry as a Lieutenant Colonel, on duty in the Jersies and afterwards in Virginia and Carolina. He probably returned to New York after Cornwallis' surrender at Yorktown in the Fall of 1781.[35] Not many of the young Tory ladies married British officers; this alliance was another mark of distinction for the brilliant and fashionable Rebecca, who now entered army life.

Johnson's *military* career had not always been victorious. At the end of May, 1779 the British had captured Stony Point, an American fortress on the Hudson approximately thirty-five miles north of New York and fifteen miles south of West Point. Johnson was placed in command of the force of some five hundred fifty holding the newly-enlarged and greatly strengthened fortress. But with West Point threatened, Washington laid plans for its recapture which succeeded in an extremely daring operation.

Stony Point was almost impregnable. Surrounded by water on three sides at all times, at high water it became an island. The fourth side, the only possible approach by land, was a morass, guarded by sharpened stakes and other traps. But only six weeks after the British had taken the fort General Anthony Wayne and his men advanced from a point some fourteen miles below the fortress by moving over crags and through defiles in single file up close to it. From there they were guided by a black slave. Just before midnight on July 15 the Americans overpowered the sentries, and silently overran the British force by bayonet. Johnson lost his right ear and afterwards always wore a ribbon over it. Wayne was wounded in the head and thought he might die, but the wound was not serious and he was able to take the surrender of Colonel Johnson and his men. Ironically, it was Colonel Jack Stewart, Rebecca's admirer, who led the Maryland troops in the assault on the fort commanded by her future husband.[36] Such were the civilities of war in those days that after the fall of the fort Johnson wrote directly to Washington and received permission for certain of his officers to go to New York for necessaries for the captured garrison—"The strictest attention being paid to the time limited for their return."[37]

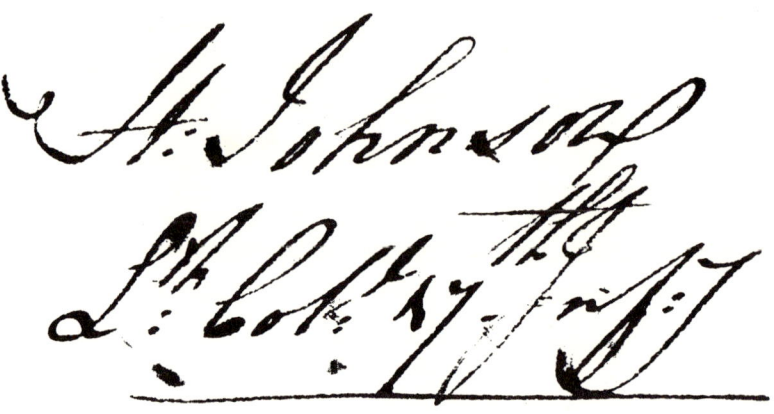

David Franks' letters from New York indicate that in the May after their marriage the Johnsons returned to England, where they seem promptly to have settled at Bath. A publication by one Cantelo, "Musician at Bath," in 1785 collected "Twenty Four American Country Dances as Danced by the British during their Winter Quarters at Philadelphia, New York and Charlestown." One of these was titled "Mrs. Lt. Col: Johnsons Reel."[38] In that same year Rebecca spunkily recrossed the ocean, accompanying her husband when the 17th Infantry under his command was ordered to Nova Scotia and Newfoundland. Rebecca gave birth to their first son, Henry Allen, in Shelbourne, Nova Scotia, on September 26, 1785.

At the time of England's war with France, Johnson was sent to Ireland and given command of three thousand men at New Ross, where in pitched battle he defeated the Irish rebels in June, 1798 in the hardest fighting of the rebellion. After serving as governor of New Ross Castle, in 1809 he became a full General, and in 1818 he was created a Baronet.[39]

The beautiful Rebecca had her portrait painted in England at an early age, in what appears to be the same gown in which she had triumphed at the Mischianza Ball in Philadelphia in 1778. The portrait presents a highly intelligent face. Her gown is of white silk, open in the front to the waist. At the Ball it was set off by a towering jeweled headdress, for on that occasion Rebecca had been attended by a court of six ladies and crowned one of two "Queens of Beauty."

In 1810 a gentleman who visited the Johnsons at Bath gave an account of Rebecca, later published by Elizabeth Ellet:

> She was living in elegant style, and exercising with characteristic grace the duties of hospitality and the virtues that adorn social life. He described her person as of the middle height, rather inclining to the embonpoint, and her expression of countenance is very agreeable, with fine eyes. Her manners are frank and cheerful, and she appeared happy in contributing to the happiness of others.[40]

Lady Johnson, née Rebecca Franks

General Winfield Scott's interview with Rebecca at Bath in 1816 has been recorded in full in his memoirs.[41] He was still only thirty and fresh from his triumphs on the Canadian border in the War of 1812. Arriving at her home, he presented an introductory letter "from a belle of Philadelphia to her great aunt, Lady J., wife of Sir Henry Johnson, Baronet, residing at Bath, and a senior general of the British Army." Scott seems to have been anxious to meet Rebecca because of her writing the satirical poem of 1779. In his words:

> This lady, in 1779, and some years before, was, as Miss Franks, the belle of Philadelphia—handsome, witty and an heiress. She was also high in toryism and eccentricity. Many amusing sarcasms of hers, leveled at revolutionary men of eminence, were in circulation in Philadelphia down to the autobiographer's early days.

Scott vividly recorded the meeting, which he wrote "at this distant day cannot be recalled without emotion." Nor can it now. At this time Rebecca, age fifty-eight, had suffered the death of George, her second son and an infantry Captain, in Spain four years earlier:[42]

> In 1816 she had become, from bad health, prematurely old—a very near approach to a ghost, but with eyes still bright, and other remains of her former self.
> On the receipt of the letter of introduction, Lady J. despatched her amiable husband—a fine old soldier, to fetch the stranger . . . . She had been rolled out in an easy chair to receive him [Scott was writing in the third person]. On presentation, he was transfixed by her eager, but kindly gaze. "Is this the young rebel!" were her first words. "My dear, it is your countryman," etc., said Sir Henry, fearing that Scott might take offence. "Yes, it is," she quickly added, "the young rebel; and you have taken the liberty to beat his majesty's troops." Scott, by a pleasant word or two, parried the impeachment as well as he could; but the lady followed up the accusation, with specific references, which surprised not a little. Scott soon found himself seated by her side, with a hand clasped in both of hers—cold and clammy, as in the article of death. Taking a sudden turn, she exclaimed, with emphasis: "I have gloried in my rebel countrymen!" Then pointing to heaven, with both hands, she added, in a most affecting tone: "Would to God I, too, had been a patriot." A gentle remonstrance was interposed by the husband, who had been carried away by sympathy up to this moment.

Home of Lady Johnson, née Rebecca Franks – Catharine Place, Bath

Turning now upon him, she said, with the earnestness of truth: "I do not, I have never regretted my marriage. No woman was ever blessed with a kinder, a better husband; but I ought to have been a patriot before marriage." Hers were the only dry eyes of the party.

The house in which General Scott was received still stands in Bath—the house given as Rebecca's address at the time of her death from a "decline" and "after a severe trial" seven years later in February, 1823 at the age of sixty-four.[43] It was now more than forty years since her escapades and exhibitions of wit during the Revolution, when she was so fully committed to the British cause. Presumably Rebecca never saw Woodford again after she sorrowfully left it in November, 1780. She was buried in the graveyard, now obliterated and used for a hotel and car park, of old St. Michael's,[44] Bath. Her family was now well established there, for her son lived there and her grandson had been born there in 1819. Her husband lived on until 1835 and died at the age of eighty-eight.

VI
Thomas Paschall,
David Hayfield Conyngham,
William Lewis

The way in which Thomas Paschall acquired Woodford seems to have characterized his relationship with it for the next thirteen years. He had not sought it out with the idea of buying it for family use—he took it because it was available to serve as part payment of the indebtedness of someone he might never see again. It was a business matter and he appears consistently to have let it remain so. There is no record of his ever living at Woodford.

The property was still subject to the first lien of Barclay's mortgage given in 1769 to Coleman's estate. This was long overdue, and could bring about a total loss of Paschall's investment if foreclosed. Although during the War there was no market for the sale of country homes, rental for income remained possible. Here, then, was an available method for a practical merchant to pay off the mortgage. He undoubtedly saw an advertisement in the *Pennsylvania Packet* for the rental of a house of much lesser stature—a farm house—within six months of his owning Woodford, on May 8, 1781:

> To be let,
> For the Summer season, or longer, and may be entered on immediately, A very
> Pleasant, healthy Country House,
> Situate near the four mile stone, on the Falls road, opposite to David Franks country seat; it has two rooms on a floor with a piazza round it, well furnished; also a Kitchen, a milk

house, and a Stable adjoining, and a pump of good water at the door. Enquire of Thomas Armet, grocer, in Second Street, below the corner of Market Street.
N.B. It is in a very good neighborhood, and near many principal country seats.

When Paschall succeeded in obtaining his first tenant is unknown, but he succeeded in less than a year and a half, under war conditions of interrupted trade, in paying the full mortgage debt with interest for seven hundred seven pounds.[1] Now he could relax for any necessary further period until a buyer could be found.

These conclusions as to Paschall's approach to Woodford are strongly supported by the fact that he had no family who would enjoy a summer place. Born in 1722,[2] he was already fifty-eight when he took title. He had married Ann Chandler at Philadelphia Meeting in 1746. Their three sons had died at tender years, and Ann herself in the spring of 1779.[3] Paschall's business interests now occupied his time.

His family, and through them his friends and acquaintances, were numerous and long established in the Society of Friends. His great grandfather Thomas had become a settler in his latter forties, apparently before the arrival of William Penn, in order to take up a purchase from Penn of five hundred unseen acres lying in today's Southwest Philadelphia, west of the Schuylkill. The area was long called Pascallville[4] and extended along the Darby Road (now Woodland Avenue) from the neighborhood of the University of Pennsylvania to beyond the Church of St. James Kingsessing. By 1684 he had cleared six acres from the virgin forest and was able to resume his business as a pewterer. He was the first such in Philadelphia. At the time of Penn's arrival Paschall the emigrant had had thirty years in the trade following upon his apprenticeship to *his* father, who was also a pewterer in Bristol, England. The settler had built a log cabin on his property and seen that in 1682 his name was entered on the first list of "Coopers, House Carpenters, etc.," in Philadelphia.[5]

In 1683 Thomas Paschall the emigrant wrote a well-known letter to a friend back home which, because of its descriptions and phrases such as "I never wisht myself at Bristol again since my departure," was printed in London as an aid in Penn's real estate promotions of his colony. There were "an infinite number of small fish in sholes, also large fish leaping in the Water." English farmers along the Delaware enjoyed "as good bread and drank as good drink as ever I did in England." Prices in general were almost impossibly low. Imported English goods were sold at "very reasonable rates." Much interior land did not even require clearing, and the Indians preferred the English settlers over other whites. William Penn had arrived, was "well approved of," and "behaved himself as Noble."[6]

Paschall did his share in public affairs. He was a member of the Assembly of the Colony in 1685, 1689 and 1717. Under Philadelphia's first charter of 1691 he was named one of the town's twelve councilmen. In 1705 he served on a committee which first divided the city into wards.[7]

Although Paschall the emigrant had apprenticed his son Thomas to his trade in England, that son, the grandfather of Woodford's owner, was of independent mind. In the new world he became a malt and barley dealer[8] and established himself farther up the Schuylkill at Blockley, extending north of Market Street and in part in the area of present-day Fairmount Park.[9] He acted also as a tax assessor for lands beyond the Schuylkill. This Thomas had at least eleven children, most of them boys and one of them Thomas, apparently the father of Thomas of Woodford. They spread into numerous livelihoods, with businesses associated with metals common. Some had contrasting avocations. One was the first volunteer fireman in Philadelphia,[10] and another a member of the Schuylkill Fishing Company.

Thomas, owner of Woodford, was born in Goshen, Chester County, for his father had married a Goshen resident, Margaret Jones, and moved there.[11] Thomas was a hatter at the time of his marriage[12] but upon obtaining capital became a merchant in iron, listed in the early city directories as an "ironmonger" located at 25 North Second Street, in the same block as Christ Church.[13] He was resolute in his opposition to enforcement of the Stamp Act and signed the local merchants' Non-Importation Agreement of 1765.[14] His ledger for the resale of bar iron bought at wholesale is extant for the years 1767 to 1770.[15] As a Quaker non-combatant he remained in Philadelphia during the British occupation, for he signed the agreement of numerous local merchants to accept the Colonial paper money in lieu of specie.[16] Just what he bought and sold during that time is unknown, but the British would not have

Thomas Paschall of Philad.ᵃ Ironmonger aged 69

The Historical Society of Pennsylvania

permitted him to traffic in commodities helpful to the Revolutionary authorities. He maintained a low profile as a neutral, and after the return of the Patriots found himself able on August 27, 1778 to take the oath of allegiance to the new Commonwealth of Pennsylvania.[17]

If not then, certainly later he dealt not only in iron objects, but also in steel and brass, and must have imported much of his stock in trade. The inventory filed in his estate in 1796[18] listed many fascinating items: 97 gross small screws, 48 gross "larger screws," 7 dozen "Chizzells," 4 dozen and 4 closet locks, 31 shoemaker's cramping hammers and 14 dozen shoemaker's awls, 4 dozen and 11 rasps and files, 29 Dutch cooper axes, 10 dozen and 11 brass bookcase locks, and watchmaker's files, tea table catches, fish hooks, saws and pulleys!

But Paschall was more of a standard link in the chain of Woodford than at first appears. Like Coleman, he left no wife or children. Like Coleman, he was a friend of Benjamin Franklin— who was a witness at Paschall's wedding.[19] Like all the earlier owners of Woodford, he was a merchant. Not only did he have business dealings with Franks (from whom he received other real estate in addition to Woodford), his predecessor in the Woodford title, but also with Isaac Wharton, his successor in it.

Paschall died March 28, 1796, and by will[20] named his cousin Christopher Marshall, Junior, to settle his estate. He remembered in his will nieces and nephews, cousins of various degrees, sisters-in-law, a brother-in-law, friends, and eight persons in his service including a negro boy, Cato. In his lengthy provisions he left approximately six thousand pounds in cash gifts to relatives plus lands in Pennsylvania and New Jersey and many silver objects, along with his residuary estate. His housekeeper and assistant, who had given "years of attention to my affairs of trade," received "2700 Spanish milled silver dollars," lands in Pennsylvania, and much silver including "my newest Cream Pot with the Paschall family arms." To his other servitors he gave three hundred pounds. He even remembered to include a gift to the young Pennsylvania Hospital.

Perhaps all of Paschall's tenants at Woodford are not known; but there may have been only two.

David Hayfield Conyngham, a Revolutionary soldier, was Thomas's tenant at Woodford in 1783—the year of the peace. Conyngham's occupancy of the mansion adds a colorful and substantial personality to the list of those associated with it.

He was born in Philadelphia in 1750 and educated first at the Academy of Philadelphia and later for two years at Trinity College, Dublin. His father had come to Philadelphia from Ireland and before David's birth had established a shipping house prominent from 1745 until after 1880.

Conyngham early became convinced of the rightness of the American cause and in 1774, while David Franks was enjoying Woodford at the high point of his career, became one of a Philadelphia corps of volunteers under Captain John Cadwalader. After joining his father's firm in the following year, Conyngham went abroad on one of the firm's ships. During the voyage he was captured by pirates but managed to escape and proceed to Paris where he signed on for a privateering voyage. When the French authorities learned of this, they were bent upon Conyngham's arrest. It was only through the offices of his father's great friend, Benjamin Franklin, that Conyngham escaped the Bastille. The two became friends. Upon his release Conyngham went to Bordeaux where he purchased medical stores for General Washington. He did not return home until 1779 and then did so by way of the West Indies. On this voyage, despite a second shipwreck, he returned safely to Philadelphia. Now he promptly saw active duty in the Revolutionary forces in the latter part of 1779.[21]

On October 4 Conyngham, in military uniform, was walking near Third and Walnut Streets, Philadelphia, when he found himself precipitated into what has since been known as the "Battle of Fort Wilson." On the corner of those streets stood the home of James Wilson, one of the signers of the Declaration of Independence, but also an attorney who had ventured to defend Tories on trial as traitors. Spirits ran high at this time because it was considered that action against the Tories was not sufficiently severe. A mob including many militia privates was formed which voiced in advance an intention to storm Wilson's home and harm him. A group of his friends assembled in the house for defense. The discharge, or perhaps only the display, of a pistol from the house acted to detonate the short fuse of the crowd of two hundred armed ruffians. Vindictive and bloodthirsty, they made the assault, using two cannons as well. On both sides a number were wounded. A few were killed. Conyngham entered the house to help, just in time to see a Continental officer fall dead on the stairs, shot from an outside cellar window. Mounted members of the First City Troop suddenly appeared. Using swords freely, they broke up the riot, and arrested many. The incident was long remembered and discussed.[22]

In June, 1780 Conyngham was on active duty in New Jersey, and in January, 1781 in connection with the revolt of the Pennsylvania troops. But it is known that in June, 1783 he was renting Woodford as a country seat, for he then returned home to unexpected visitors. Perhaps one hundred disbanded soldiers of the Pennsylvania Line had marched from Lancaster and descended that day upon the State House, intent upon obtaining redress for their failure to receive back pay due them. Under the command of sergeants they presented themselves before the State House, drawn up in formation in the street. Although they made no effort to enter the building or to insult the Congress, its members became very much alarmed and at once adjourned to meet at Princeton. When Conyngham returned to Woodford he found that Mr. and Mrs. Robert Morris had fled there in the excitement. They stayed at Woodford until the alarm abated, which Conyngham said "they were sorry they had dreaded."[23]

The wide-ranging Conyngham left Woodford at an unknown date, had Louis Phillipe, King of France, as his houseguest,[24] lost another country house by fire, and built still another which still stands not very far from Woodford on the Germantown Road.[25] It is the headquarters of the Germantown Historical Society.

There is a strong tradition, and numerous authors have flatly stated, that during the thirteen years of Paschall's ownership Woodford was also rented for a time to William Lewis.[26] Lewis was a most active and highly regarded member of the Philadelphia Bar—a Quaker born in 1751 and reared in Chester County; a picturesque and very strong character, and a celebrated lawyer. He was the third attorney to be admitted to practice in the new Commonwealth of Pennsylvania, in September, 1777. During the occupation he retired to the county of his birth; but he returned after departure of the British. Strictly within his profession Lewis' high points came when Washington appointed him United States Attorney for the District of Pennsylvania in September, 1789 and when beginning in 1791 he served as a judge appointed by Washington to the first Federal District Court, sitting in Philadelphia. He was a close friend and adviser to Washington and a Federalist member of the Pennsylvania legislature. Lewis is most remembered for having framed the first legislative measure for gradual emancipation of the slaves—a measure which as a member of the legislative Assembly he was instrumental in having become the law of Pennsylvania in 1780.[27]

Lewis, an inveterate cigar smoker and a very tall man whose remarkable nose was an additional reason for his physical prominence, lived for many years at Fort Wilson, site of the 1779 riot and siege. He was wont in warm weather to walk back and forth before the house, bareheaded, always puffing a cigar.[28]

Lewis became enamored of the property adjoining Woodford to the north. Now, much changed and enlarged, it is known as Strawberry Mansion; at that time it contained a somewhat ruined farmhouse and out-buildings. In 1783 he purchased it with the intent to improve it. The exact date when Lewis began his remodelling and restoration of the house which now forms the central part of Strawberry Mansion is not known, but the work is believed to have been completed by the end of the 1780s. Lewis could well have rented Woodford during the time that he was rebuilding the next-door farmhouse for his family then living in town at Third and Walnut Streets. Although the site was only four miles from Philadelphia, living at Woodford would have enabled Lewis to avoid the repeated trips necessary to follow the progress of his project, at the same time allowing him more direct supervision of it. It has been said that Washington, in the years of his first term as president, with Philadelphia the national capital, visited Lewis at Woodford for consultation on political subjects.[29] If so, Lewis's tenancy extended to 1790 and beyond, perhaps until Paschall's sale of Woodford on August 28, 1793.[30]

Until about that time the postwar economy remained depressed and business slow. But the property was finally sought for its own sake by the Isaac Whartons. With their children and grandchildren they would continue in it for the longest period of any private ownership.

VII
Seventy-Five Years of
Wharton Family Ownership

Woodford now fetched twenty-two hundred fifty pounds. Although its new owner, Isaac Wharton, was already forty-eight, he had married only seven years earlier and had four small children ranging in age from five to a baby of four months.[1] He and his wife Margaret Rawle (fifteen years his junior) appear to have promptly made changes in the interior arrangements of the mansion.

Experts opine that certain of the interior woodwork was installed in the period around 1800, when the two original bedrooms on the north side of the first floor were remodeled into one large room matching in size the original south-side parlor, and what had been two bedrooms over the parlor as installed by David Franks became only one large room also matching the downstairs parlor in size. At Isaac's death in 1808 an inventory of furnishings at Woodford[2] disclosed that both the large front rooms downstairs contained "dining" tables of mahogany but that the north room (the present dining room) was apparently the one used for meals because it contained a sideboard and knife-box—the south room being equipped more for serving tea on two tea tables. The north room also boasted a sofa but contained no chairs. Five chairs were listed in the hallway and seven windsors in the south parlor.

Upstairs, all space was put to use for bedrooms: one bedstead, a desk and two chairs in what is now the master bedroom;

another bed, two chairs and a child's chair in what is now the nursery; two beds and two mahogany bureaus in the present "maple living room;" and two more beds and another mahogany bureau in the second floor west room with its panelled wall and fireplace; even two beds in the garret. By 1808 there were five children in the family—the oldest age twenty and the youngest, Rebecca, about thirteen.

Oil of Woodford by unknown artist marked "1799" on reverse

Five years after acquiring Woodford, Isaac bought ten more acres of adjoining ground fronting on the Wissahickon Road, nearly doubling the area of his holdings and extending the south boundary to front on Macpherson's Lane.[3] This ran from the Wissahickon Road in a direct line to Mt. Pleasant Mansion overlooking the Schuylkill, and served several other residences. Obtaining double frontage may have been Isaac's motive; but the new lot appears to have come on the market at quite advantageous terms at that time. Joshua Howell, who had bought it in 1760 as a part of the breakup of Joseph Shute's lands, had died, leaving the lot to his son-in-law Johns Hopkins. Hopkins promptly offered it for sale.[4] Wharton paid only fifty pounds per acre, and indeed seems to have acquired Woodford from Paschall on bargain terms also. Paschall sold for only slightly more, or possibly even less, than the value he had given David Franks. Including the old mortgage of five hundred pounds which Paschall paid, he allowed Franks eighteen hundred thirty pounds. After inflation had further reduced currency values, Paschall received from Wharton thirteen years after purchase only twenty-two hundred and fifty.

At first blush it might seem peculiar that Isaac bought Woodford at all, because a country seat near the city, which had been well known to Rebecca Franks, was already available in the Wharton family. Isaac was one of eighteen children of Joseph Wharton, who retired in his later years from the city to a substantial country home only perhaps two miles distant in Southwark, known as Walnut Grove. Joseph died in the summer of 1776.[5] In his will he failed to bequeath Walnut Grove explicitly but directed that, after a period of leasing, his residuary lands be divided equally among his children by six impartial persons.[6] This was accomplished in 1789. But by that time the city was rapidly spreading into the area. Joseph's property had extended from at least Sixth Street on the west to the Delaware on the east, but now new streets were being plotted through it on the grid pattern used in the old city. The partition was made on the basis of these new streets. On a handsome plan of the area which Isaac commissioned,[7] he is shown as having received the block bounded by Fifth, Sixth, Washington and Federal Streets which included the mansion and its flanking buildings. But a part of the main house stood in the line of the new Fifth Street and one of the smaller buildings protruded into the intersection of the new Fifth and new Washington Streets. City building lots were on the way. Indeed the condition of the mansion was probably poor, for it had been vacant in May, 1778 when the British commandeered it for the Mischianza Ball and used it for the necessities of that occasion, and it had probably been mistreated when the Patriots returned to the city and regarded it as polluted. It quickly acquired the reputation of a "haunted house," and later became a poor-children's asylum, a coach factory, and a public school.[8]

On the other hand, the bride whom Wharton married at the Bank Meeting House in Philadelphia had grown up at her parents' country seat known as Laurel Hill, next door to Woodford; and she longed to return for the summers to the country area she knew. Margaret Rawle's letters written from the city, where she was forced to remain in 1776, show her predilection for country living. Writing to her friend Sally Wister in Germantown in the heat of July she said:

> How agreeable your Situation, and how much the reverse is mine. You out of the noise of the town in the coole, the silent shades,— an agreeable company very near, Sweet walks; you enjoy these Charming Moonlight evenings. For my part I never was so lonesome in my life as I am now. I set at the door by myself, not a Creature to speak to.

In September of the same year another letter to Sally was more specific:

> May the Pleasures of the town be equal to those of the Country, is the kind wish you close your letter with; but that cannot be to one who Prefers the Country so much to the town as I do. I almost envy every boddy that is agreeably situated in the Country, nor is it to be wondered at since I Past some of the most agreeable Parts of my Life at Laurel Hill. Nine or ten Summers I Past there, the Remembrance of which is still dear to me, and makes me regret Passing them any where el's.[9]

With very young children, the Isaac Whartons would have seen the need to escape for the summer from the heat, noxious odors and diseases of the city. What more natural than to think in terms of the Laurel Hill area of fashionable seats along the Schuylkill? They both knew Thomas Paschall, the owner of Woodford—and knew him well, for he had signed their wedding certificate in Quaker fashion as a witness to their marriage.[10] Paschall was ready to sell. The combination of circumstances was fortuitous. And Margaret was still only turning thirty-three at the time of the purchase: more children could be expected, and in fact a daughter was born two years later.

Paschall was not the only person with ties to Woodford who had attended the wedding of Margaret and Isaac. From the early days of Coleman's ownership there was his nephew, George Clymer, who had known the mansion so well as a child. Numerous Whartons also were witnesses to the marriage. Of them Robert, Isaac's half brother, was to become first a member of the City Council, then Alderman of the city, and still later Mayor of Philadelphia for five terms.[11] Isaac himself was to be elected to the City Council in 1791, before the years of his brother's service. He had also served as a Manager of the Pennsylvania Hospital for a term ending shortly after his marriage.[12]

Isaac was a merchant, like others of his family, and also a marine insurance broker. He seems to have had no desire for prominence in the War years. He remained in Philadelphia as a neutral during the British occupation of 1777-1778 and appeared in the signature of the firm of himself and his brother, as a party to the agreement to accept the Continental paper money—"Thomas and Isaac Wharton". On October 16, 1779 he took the oath of allegiance to Pennsylvania within a few days of two of his brothers.[13]

This was no step to be taken lightly. The general militia law of June, 1777 had required such an oath. In the form of affirmation taken by Isaac he first renounced his allegiance to George III, then undertook to bear true allegiance to Pennsylvania as a free and independent state, agreeing to do nothing prejudicial or injurious to it. But there was another part of the oath which caused many to refuse the whole of it: a sworn agreement to inform on any other person whose act of disloyalty might come to the knowledge of the swearer. Yet by the terms of this stringent law those who refused or neglected to take the oath could not hold office, serve on juries, sue for debts, vote, or be elected, buy or sell real estate, be armed, or leave their city or county except subject to arrest as spies.[14] Isaac brought his conscience to accept the obligation to inform on others.

His first business venture appears to have been as a merchant in partnership with his older brother Thomas before the Revolution approached Philadelphia. Thomas was of great wealth and influence. Until the War he was a Patriot who corresponded with Benjamin Franklin. But when the colonies took up arms he changed his sympathies. He became one of some forty prominent Philadelphia Quakers whom the authorities arrested in September, 1777, marched to Virginia, and kept in exile there until the following Spring; later his property was confiscated.[15] By 1782 Thomas had died and Isaac was referring to "the *late* office of Thos. & Isaac Wharton". The firm had, at least in part, engaged in marine insurance and until the Fall of 1776 it had held the active account of David Franks.[16]

By 1785 "Isaac and Samuel Wharton" were listed as a firm of merchants and insurance brokers. Isaac was now in business with a Patriot older brother who was a friend of Franklin and had served in the Continental Congress toward the end of the war.[17]

Although beginning in 1795 Isaac was listed for his remaining years simply as a merchant and not as a member of a partnership, he was also President of the Phoenix Insurance Company, at least after 1800,[18] and in his will of 1802[19] referred to his partnership with David Lewis as "Wharton and Lewis," engaged in land speculation. This continued until his death in 1808.

Despite Isaac's increasing the extent of Woodford and remodeling parts of the interior, it seems hardly likely that the property was more than a summer retreat for his family. He had a fine double house in the city on North Front Street until 1796—so splendid that it was said to be "a guarantee of the wealth and dignity" of its owner.[20] He then moved to a new home and in his will left to his wife for her life "my new house in which I now live in this city . . . I trust she will live with my children in my said new house." For commuting to Woodford, he left a coach, a carriage, and a "chair." His listing as a merchant at Third Street in 1808 indicates that he remained an active businessman in town, and he died in that year in his early sixties. No portrait of Isaac is known, but Margaret's was painted by Sully in 1825 when she was sixty-five.[21]

Isaac provided by will that when his oldest child should reach twenty-one, "five responsible and discreet persons" should partition the real estate he left in equal shares to his children. Woodford was allotted to his oldest child Francis Rawle Wharton, who became owner by deed of August 21, 1809, signed seven months after he reached maturity.[22] Isaac bequeathed to his wife "all the plate, books, furniture and other articles in my dwelling houses in the city and in the country at Woodford". The mansion may nonetheless have remained furnished after his death as it was earlier, for Margaret lived until the age of seventy-one in 1831. Before the transfer of title Isaac's estate paid "for work at Woodford", presumably repairs; and in 1810 it subscribed for stock in the new Ridge Road Turnpike Company.[23]

Francis followed in his father's footsteps both by making his business career as a merchant (later a real estate broker) and by waiting until mature years to marry. Isaac had married at forty-one. Francis waited seventeen years after receiving Woodford to marry at thirty-eight. His bride, Juliana Matilda Gouverneur, was from New York City.

Francis held title to the mansion for fifty-three years, and it remained in his estate for another seven—thus completing sixty years after Isaac's tenure of fifteen and making seventy-five years of continuous, if uneventful, ownership in one family.

Francis was truly of a new generation as regards Woodford. He had been born in 1788 and was its first owner in almost forty years who had not experienced the Revolutionary War. And he helped bring Woodford into the city. Acting probably in the hope of improvements for the Northern Liberties area, and out of shock at the riots of 1844, Francis signed a petition to call a town meeting held in November, 1849 to consider the proposed consolidation of the city and its outlying districts.[24] This major change took place in 1854, when Woodford became for the first time a part of the City of Philadelphia.

Presumably Francis' mother and his brothers and 'sisters— the youngest, Rebecca, was just reaching fourteen when the property was deeded to him in 1809—continued to use Woodford in the summers after Francis took title. But still there was apparently no year-round occupancy. As had his father, Francis always maintained a house in the city. At the same time there is evidence that summer activity continued at Woodford. The property was increased by new farm buildings which are shown on maps prepared later upon purchase by the city for inclusion in Fairmount Park. The "new" ten acres had already contained a wooden barn when acquired. It and the later additions imply rental of the overall acreage to a farmer or farm superintendent for

Mrs. Isaac Wharton, née Margaret Rawle, age 65 (1825)

an operating farm. Apparently Woodford escaped the fate of others of the Fairmount Park mansion properties: a number of them, particularly those close along the banks of the Schuylkill, were abandoned during these years because of the "river fever." The occupants of the riverside estates realized that it was only after completion of the Fairmount Dam in 1822 that many became seriously ill of "river fever" and in numerous cases died during the summer months. But they did not know the cause. The damming of the free-flowing river had for the first time created pools of sluggish water in which mosquitoes multiplied.[25] They were contracting yellow fever. There is nothing to indicate, however, that Woodford, a quarter-mile from the stream, was ever closed. After Francis' brothers and sisters matured, his own children—five boys and two girls—were born beginning in the late 1820's and provided strong reasons for retaining and using the country home. Alfred, the youngest child, was born in 1839. There were, too, the children of Francis' brother Thomas Isaac, a lawyer, and of his sister Rebecca Smith, who must have enjoyed the old house.

Thus the Wharton family lived quietly at Woodford through the very rapid expansion of Philadelphia in the first half of the nineteenth century and through the momentous events of United States history culminating in the Civil War. The property was still a summer home and probably under lease as an operating farm. The steady development of North Philadelphia into blocks of row homes never physically reached the area; Francis never experienced at Woodford the kind of urban surge which had overtaken Walnut Grove. He died during the war in February, 1862 at the age of seventy-four, leaving a will of the preceding year in which he left the property to his children.[26] There had been seven, and in 1863 there were still five. Francis' widow lived on until March, 1870 and would be expected to be at the mansion in the summers. Once again, continuity of ownership indicated that things would continue as they had for so many uninterrupted years.

VIII
The Fairmount Park Period

Unexpectedly, however, the year 1867 saw the first of a series of outside events which would quickly change the course of Woodford's history. In that year the Pennsylvania legislature expanded the borders of "Fairmount Park" and set up for the first time a Fairmount Park Commission to administer the enlarged acreage and its structures.[1]

What was to become Fairmount Park had actually commenced as early as 1812 when five acres of land had been acquired for a works to conduct pure water from the Schuylkill into the city. Upon it the Fairmount Water Works was erected in 1815.[2] Throughout the first half of the 1800s public concern grew steadily for preserving the Schuylkill as a source of unadulterated water for Philadelphians. Petitions were circulated and pamphlets published on the subject;[3] but more than that, groups of public-spirited citizens used their own funds to see that properties draining into the river near the city were acquired and removed as sources of pollution.[4] The first of these was Lemon Hill, slightly upstream from the Fairmount works, which had fallen from one of the City's showplaces embellished by handsome and famous gardens to a mansion in ruinous condition surrounded by overrun and neglected grounds. In 1844 this forty-five acre property was bought by the city; and in 1855 it was officially designated as "Fairmount Park"—largely because the area had become part of

101

Philadelphia a year earlier by the Consolidation Act which mandated parks in the expanded city.[5] The acquisition of Sedgley by a group of citizen trustees who gave title to the city in 1857, extended the acquired area across Girard Avenue and the acreage by thirty-four.[6] This was also dedicated to the public use.

In the 1860s the properties amassed for pure water purposes were still interspersed with many industrial and business structures, particularly on the banks of the river between the Fairmount Water Works and Lemon Hill, but also farther upstream. Thus it was that in 1867 the legislature settled matters by ordaining a specified "Fairmount Park" extending upstream beyond Girard Avenue, establishing a Commission to administer the enlarged area, and providing damages for the taking of properties lying within the new outer boundaries.

Even this action did not touch Woodford, for it still lay outside. The property continued undisturbed in the hands of the Wharton heirs, although by this time "paper" streets had been extended through it and the other properties on the river side of 33rd Street. One such cut off the front of the mansion house.[7] Upon a grid map it appeared that the property was split into several separate segments—a valuable investment for a developer in building homes fronting on these various streets if they should become a reality.

Instead, the new Park Commission quickly became concerned from the water purity standpoint with the small size of the area appropriated to its jurisdiction. It went to City Council, which secured from the legislature a further Act in April, 1868[8] greatly extending the 1867 boundaries of the Park[9]—in Woodford's area to 33rd Street. Any paper streets disappeared. Now Woodford was a part of Fairmount Park.

The Commission made every effort to pay for the private properties brought within the boundaries by reaching voluntary agreements with the owners. Thus in March, 1869 deeds were given to the City of Philadelphia by the children of Francis R. Wharton for Woodford.[10] A small corner of its twenty-two acres, lying between 33rd Street and Ridge Avenue, still lay outside the Park boundary. For this about thirty-five hundred dollars was received. The remainder, including the buildings, now commanded a price of more than forty-six thousand five hundred dollars.

Some of the structures lying within the Park were removed by the Park Commission, which had promptly instructed the Captain of its newly-appointed police or "guards" to report "in detail the condition of all houses, stables and structures made of brick, wood, stone, exact position, name of occupant, excepting large buildings such as Memorial Hall, and recommend any which he [the Captain] considered should be demolished."[11] Removal was the fate of businesses and industries as well as of some of the old residences in the Park;[12] but Woodford was spared, undoubtedly because of its architectural quality and the enduring strength and generally good condition of the structure. The *Third Annual Report of the Commissioners of Fairmount Park* included mention of the fact that:

> The Mansion at Woodford, situated on the Ridge Avenue front of the East Park, probably one of the oldest family seats in the Park, was put in repair and designated as the residence of the Chief Engineer, by whom it has been occupied since the close of September [1870].[13]

Woodford's continuance was assured.

John C. Cresson was the Chief Engineer and Superintendent of Fairmount Park who occupied Woodford.[14] He was highly qualified for his position. Born in Philadelphia in 1806, he had already had a distinguished career. His education included emphasis on the sciences. After being given a farm by his father and making a try at farm life, he returned to the city and entered upon a close relationship with the Franklin Institute by displaying a comprehensive knowledge of mechanics and chemistry. He was active as an academic professor and as superintendent of the newly-built City Gas Works. During later life he served on numerous boards of directors, both charitable and business, and was elected Senior Vice President of the American Philosophical Society. He was also President of the Franklin Institute. Finally, he was appointed by the Board of Judges as one of the original Commissioners of Fairmount Park; and in that capacity he agreed to serve as its first Chief Engineer and Superintendent. Among his early programs was one for the topographical mapping of the East Park (i.e. lying upstream from Girard Avenue). The *Second Annual Report of the Commissioners* mentioned preparation of such a map for the area "near Ridge Avenue on the Wharton tract."[15] His early love for rural surroundings and pursuits came to the fore in planning the arrangement of the Park.

The David Kennedy watercolor of Woodford now on display in its old kitchen dates from the 1870s, perhaps during Cresson's occupancy. It is a sunny rendering from a distance of the mansion with its tawny brick color.

Fairmount Park Commission. Philadelphia

Watercolor of Woodford by David Kennedy—1870's

Cresson resigned in ill health in June, 1875 and was succeeded in that month by Russell Thayer, whose engineering skills were acquired at West Point. Thayer was in his early twenties when he assumed his new responsibilities. He married in 1876 and brought his bride to Woodford, where their first son was later born and where they lived until 1884. His descendants tell the story that young Mrs. Thayer, who rode side-saddle,—returning to Woodford on horseback with her husband at night by toll road and finding the toll gate closed—simply jumped the barrier while the gatekeeper slept.[16]

Thayer continued in his duties as Chief Engineer and Superintendent for nearly twenty-three years during the Park's important formative period. He was very active in relations with the Centennial Commission in the completion of the Centennial buildings as well as their later removal; he surveyed the course of the Wissahickon Creek within the Park; he designed the first public boat house on the river-front; and he was responsible for installing the river wall and shore drives.[17]

The Park Commission reported that in 1876, with greatly increased usage of the Park in conjunction with the Centennial, general repairs and improvements were made throughout the East Park.[18] Presumably these were directed by Thayer but did not alter Woodford, fresh from repair for Cresson's use.

A good example of the work begun by Cresson and completed by Thayer lies in the creation of a totally new vehicular drive connecting the East Park into an integrated whole for the first time. After obtaining his topographical maps, Cresson had a line surveyed and staked which wound from the Park boundary at 33rd Street near Woodford along the crest of the hills, linking the old mansions and ending at a point overlooking the river on a bluff upstream from Girard Avenue. In a few places room was provided for passing. In the Spring of 1871 a tunnel begun the preceding Fall at the river's edge, through the living rock of Promontory Point just above Girard Avenue, was completed. Now the East River Drive along the river was extended above the Avenue for a short distance through and beyond the tunnel. What the Commissioners termed a "provisional approach to the East Park" was made by Cresson's joining the drive to a new road leaving its terminus, crossing at grade the nearby Reading Railroad tracks, which paralleled the river, and winding up to join the crestline vehicular drive. This arrangement was unchanged at Cresson's retirement, but the railroad grade crossing was dangerous. To remove this, Thayer designed two wide arches sufficient to carry the railroad across a small valley running at right angles to the river less than a half-mile upstream from the area of the grade crossing. The railroad tracks were passed over the arches and a new carriage road link was built leading to the crestline drive. It left the river at the valley, passed under the arches and wound upwards, becoming known as Fountain Green Drive.[19] The former grade crossing and provisional road were obliterated; the new roadway opened in 1886 remains unchanged today and provides a pleasant route to Woodford from center-city Philadelphia via the East River Drive.

Two years later the work of extending the East River Drive through the village of East Falls and to the mouth of the Wissahickon was completed under Thayer's supervision, giving the public access through the Park to Woodford from the north as well as from the city. With this, and with slight relocation of a portion of the East Park carriage drive to circumvent the newly-built East Park reservoir, the East Park took on its present-day aspect.

A tremendous change in Woodford followed shortly upon Thayer's leaving the property in 1884. The duties of the Park Guard had increased steadily, particularly after the Centennial. Their mission was to prevent infractions of the Park rules and regulations, and if necessary to punish wrongdoers.[20] Usage of the Park increased from about one million visits in 1870 to ten million by the mid-1880s. A headquarters became necessary for the whole East Park extending northward from Girard Avenue to the Wissahickon. In May, 1887 Woodford was designated the East Park Guard House of the Fairmount Park Guard.[21] With this change the mansion ended one hundred and thirty years of use as a residence, never to return to it, and was subjected to the harder usage of daily Park administration.

Also contributing drastically to change at Woodford was the result of a proposal by a member of the Wharton family for a fascinating business project in Fairmount Park. William Wharton, Jr. received a license in 1889 to build a passenger railway touring the Park on both the east and west sides of the Schuylkill, subject to Commission agreement on the details.[22] Wharton had been involved in the public transportation business and had built a street car line reaching the edge of the East Park on Huntingdon Street, near Strawberry Mansion. It was apparently his active operation of that venture which sparked his desire to extend the service into the Park. A new bridge across the Schuylkill in the area of Strawberry Mansion was a part of his plan. But the out-of-park line failed and was sold, and with it apparently went Wharton's interest in a park trolley line.[23]

Renewed interest by a different group of investors in 1894 led to amendments of Wharton's license and permission to assign it to a newly formed corporation, the Fairmount Park Transportation Company. It was this company which built the unusual Fairmount Park Passenger Railway which was opened for service in the West Park on November 10, 1896. It was the first and remained the longest park line in the world; its track never crossed a public road.[24]

The connection of this railway with Woodford was much greater than simply the fact that a license had been issued to a member of the Wharton family. Almost the entire line lay in the West Park, but it crossed the river and terminated its eastern end on Woodford's front lawn. The terminal was most unusual in form.

Unlike the other stations on the line, it was built in an ornate Chinese design and contained much ornamental woodwork and ironwork.[25] The passage of cars across the front of Woodford to their turnaround on the grounds blocked the front entry to the mansion.[26] An underground foot passage was accordingly built to permit entrance to it as East Park headquarters.

Primarily to carry the new railway, Strawberry Mansion Bridge was erected on high ground in 1897. The license specified that it should be both structurally sound and ornamental, and such it still is even though the old park trolleys no longer pass across it. It elicited great interest in traction circles at the time of its construction because it was one of the largest such projects then undertaken in the United States, being almost twelve hundred and fifty feet long[27] and spanning the river by four semicircular arches. In everyday use by motor traffic, it stands unaltered except for removal of the trolley rails after the railway closed in 1946.[28] The old roadbed close to the north side of Woodford is now part of the Park drives system.

Andrew Maginnis

Fairmount Park Trolley Terminal on Woodford front lawn

Thayer had joined in superintending the alignment and construction of the railway and its bridge. With the main physical features of Fairmount Park in place, he resigned on February 11, 1898. The Commissioners adopted copious resolutions concerning the influence of his initiative and supervision upon the permanent development of the Park.[29] These attested to the benefits the public received from his long years of devoted service; but the genuine affection with which Thayer was regarded was manifested by the unofficial action of his fellow workers in presenting to him a silver bowl engraved with their names as signers of the following letter engraved upon it:

Feb. 19, 1898

Gen. Russell Thayer.
Dear Sir. The undersigned in conjunction with other employees of Fairmount Park have heard with much regret of your resignation as Chief Engineer and Superintendent of Fairmount Park and sincerely hope that the change may largely increase both your own and your family's happiness and welfare. We also earnestly request the acceptance of the accompanying keepsake as a heartfelt momento of your unlimited and ever remembered kindness to us all during the years of your direction of affairs of Fairmount Park.
Your humble servants, . . .

Woodford portrayed in relief on Thayer Bowl

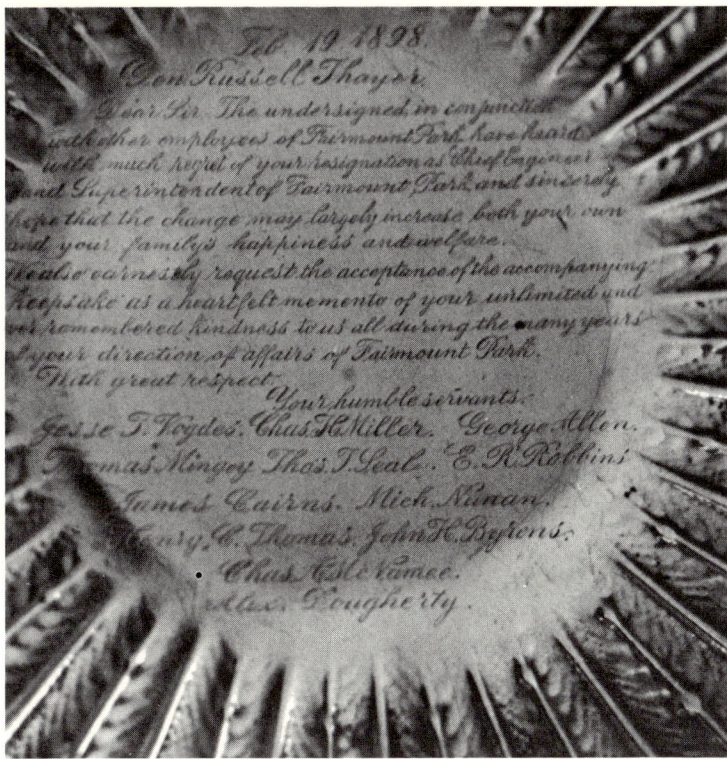

Engraving on interior of Thayer Bowl

As if this were not enough, the bowl is embellished with a front view of Woodford, one of Ridgeland, where the Thayers had also lived within the Park, and sylvan Park surroundings including two bridges.

Woodford soon saw more that was new in the Park. In 1897 and 1898 its regulations forebade automobiles, but Jules Junker dared to operate the first automobile within the Park boundaries. He was apprehended, brought to Woodford Guard House and fined for an infraction of the regulations.[30] But the incoming tide was too strong. In 1899 the operation of automobiles was first permitted, even though limited to seven miles per hour. Such a beginning was quite modest, for in that year only six hundred and ninety-six cars "passed through the Park."[31] The great concern of the Captain of the Park Guard as evinced in his report for the year was not danger to persons but rather the effect of the automobile on the greatly predominant horse traffic:

In only one instance do I find the machine was not stopped when it frightened horses. In this case the occupants went rapidly away, before the Guard reached the place. It seems to me a man versed in mechanics will have to be stationed in each District of the Park to afford relief where the machine breaks down. The standing of these machines on the drives is more calculated to frighten horses than when they are moving.[32]

The early years of this century saw the zenith of the so-called "flying squadron" of Park Police who operated by bicycle from Woodford in enforcing the speed limit. Tradition says that their sweep mustachios were almost as wide as their handlebars. Their difficulties must have increased steadily, for in 1912 more than nine hundred thousand cars used the Park roads; in 1913 almost one million two hundred thousand (a like number of vehicles counted in 1877 were carriages and sleighs); and in 1916 about three million.[33] The Commission's response to such growth came in the first of these years: on May 15, 1912 Woodford was made the Headquarters of the Park Guard and also the Traffic Court.[34] The press reported that "All official Park business and hearings will be transacted at Woodford instead of at Sedgley as formerly."

Some idea of the age of the wooded surroundings of Woodford in early days, the cluster of which clearly appears on an 1868 contour map prepared by the Park,[35] is conveyed by the work of two bolts of lightning on the grounds in the month when it became the traffic court. These forced the removal of an enormous tulip poplar tree, well known to all as "Old Pop," which stood before the mansion house. Upon examination it was found to be one hundred and ten feet high and twenty-two feet at the base. Its age was estimated at two hundred and fifty years—decades before the founding of Philadelphia. A newspaper reported, "It is said that the imposing size of the tree was responsible for the building of the Woodford Mansion near by." Its destiny became that of supplying firewood for the abused old mansion.[36] It is probably this very tree which dominates the foreground in the oil painting of the mansion which hangs in the old kitchen.

Probably because of Woodford's use for Park administration, it survived the Victorian passion for modernization and escaped any serious damage. In 1912, for its expanded functions, it was painted throughout and placed "in thorough repair." But only "minor changes were made to fit it for occupancy as the headquarters of the Park Guard."[37] A photograph from the following years shows the 1756 parlor mantelpiece largely covered by a heavy hanging oblong mirror of hardware-store type, framed in a wide painted frame and tilted strongly forward in order to make it useful. Beside it, on a panel of the recessed wall, hang handcuffs and keys suspended from pegs on a large framed board. This renders dubious the statement in secondary sources that the mantel was boarded over and in that way saved for the future. Until restoration of the mansion there appeared for business purposes to the left of the front entrance the sign "Woodford Mansion," while over the doorway the separate old sign "Woodford Guard House" was still attached beneath an overhanging electric light bulb. According to a newspaper article, "scorchers" were locked up in a "hoosegow" there.[38]

Devoted to daily service in the public interest, shorn of its original intended use, its front lawn despoiled by the railway, its stable much enlarged by sheds for the horses of the mounted Park Guards, and its servants' cottage the gathering place of the guards—but structurally intact—the old property lived on through the 1920's until the distant action of the court at Washington in the estate of Naomi Wood and approval at home by the Fairmount Park Commission, both in the early summer of 1927, gave the final seal of approval to keeping Woodford just as much in the public service but transformed into a museum illustrative of a Colonial household.

Woodford mantelpiece, handcuffs and keys, from a photograph after 1912

Philadelphia City Archives
Woodford Guard House before 1927

IX
The First Fifty Years of
The Naomi Wood Collection

The Naomi Wood trustees retained John P. B. Sinkler to supervise the restoration of Woodford Mansion. Five years younger than Daniel Huntoon, Sinkler later became the second individual trustee of the Naomi Wood Estate.

John Sinkler received his degree in architecture from the University of Pennsylvania in 1898. After four years of travel in the United States and abroad, he commenced his personal practice. He was largely responsible for the 1912 restoration of Congress Hall and rendered like services in restoring the Old City Hall. These were flanking buildings to Independence Hall, both erected in the eighteenth century. He served as President of the Philadelphia Chapter of the American Institute of Architects 1917-1918 and in the latter year was elected a Fellow of the Institute. He was City Architect from 1920 to 1924, and was still to serve as Director of the Department of City Architecture for four years.[1]

Promptly upon receipt of the court's order of approval given on June 24, 1927 came collaboration between Messrs. Huntoon and Sinkler in the necessary survey of the structure of Woodford and the determination of what repairs and changes would be made. A modern central heating system was to be introduced, for example. The preparation of the architect's drawings followed. Those extant bear date from the Fall of 1927 into that of 1928.

With the plans in hand approved by the Commissioners, work began in earnest. A news article of the period, "Old Fairmount

Park Mansion Being Restored,"[2] which described the process, commenced in the fashion of the day:

> The ghosts of an old house are awakening and rousing themselves to the changes which are coming into their abode. For Woodford is rising Phoenix-like in its new beauty—the renaissance of one of the most famous of Philadelphia's historic colonial mansions.

The reporter characterized the house as fallen into decay. "Grown out of repair, its paint peeling, cracks appearing in the mortar between its bricks, a large room on the lower floor [is] used by a series of house sergeants who know nothing of its history and care less." "The actual work of the restoration began last July after another headquarters, the old Carousel House at Forty-fourth Street and Parkside Avenue, had been chosen for the Park Guards. Assisted by Fiske Kimball and his staff from the Pennsylvania Museum, Mr. Huntoon commenced his work. Old pictures and plans of the house were unearthed to discover the original lines; . . . old paneling, hidden behind newer paneling, was uncovered; fireplaces and mantles, hidden behind partitions or entirely taken out, are being rebuilt." The article contended that Woodford's bricks had been imported from England "and are somewhat smaller than those in use today. Hence, when bricks were needed to be used for outside steps and the walls, the superintendent of the work was forced to scour the old brickyards of Philadelphia in order to find blocks of the proper size . . . Hand-fashioned beams and laths, and hand-made, wrought-iron nails were used by the original builders, and similarly tooled material is being used, wherever it will show, in the reconstruction."

The Museum's assistance mentioned by the reporter included general guidance by Fiske Kimball, research of the original paint colors by Erling H. Pedersen, his assistant, unproductive research as to the original garden by Calvin Hathaway, and later, assistance by Joseph Downs, Curator of Decorative Arts, in colors and in setting up the exhibition.[3]

Despite any implication in the press, it does not appear that any part of Woodford had been torn down or its outer lines altered except by the addition of a shed at the back. The shop drawings show that it was necessary to insert replacement pieces of wooden moldings and the like but none of the drawings indicate the substitution of entire new structural parts to the old mansion.

As the restoration approached completion, the press captioned another article "Rare Collection Gets Home In Park."[4] In this the *Public Ledger* reported that "Mr. Huntoon took great care in the redecoration of the mansion to preserve its air of antiquity, and while electric lights and radiators have been installed, they are concealed in such a manner that they will not intrude a note of modernism into the environment." Also, enthusiastically, the house "will be furnished to the last detail in the manner of Colonial Philadelphia . . . The furnishings represent various periods, as might a home in which successive generations had dwelt."

The demands on Mr. Huntoon did not end with restoration of the premises, for now came installation of the Collection into the rooms to be visited by the public. Containers of all kinds bearing Miss Wood's pieces were brought together in Memorial Hall by shipments from Massachusetts, New York and Washington. From that repository they were delivered to Woodford as their individual placement was determined upon.[5] Interest on the part of the press continued and showed a knowledge of the great variety of the items Miss Wood had left. One article reported that she had "a strong predilection for a house in Salem, Mass., and possessed a charming cottage at Gloucester; and later was swept by a marked taste for Spanish interiors and Spanish furniture."[6] It became desirable not only to use some of the foreign pieces in Mr. Huntoon's own "study" on the ground floor of Woodford (now the old kitchen), rather than for formal exhibition, but also to lend and ultimately to transfer to the Pennsylvania Museum (later the Philadelphia Museum of Art) Italian and Spanish furnishings. The Museum's Bulletins for the Fall of 1928 listed the loan to it of Italian furniture and carved figures, Persian pottery, and a Spanish chest.[7] Later it received as gifts numerous books and prints, as to which Mr. Huntoon wrote:

> Gifts from the Estate of Naomi Wood decd. to the Pennsylvania Museum of Art consisting of prints, books, etc. were made in the spirit of mutual satisfaction and accomplishment . . . The favors received from the Museum saved The Estate from actual cash expenditures. The Museum gave to The Estate the entire use of one large room in Memorial Hall for about one year, in which were unpacked over 500 cases and crates . . . The Museum also restored, by expert workmanship, free of charge, all antique furniture now on exhibition

at Woodford Mansion, Fairmount Park. This seemed to me a fair and equitable transaction.

Miss Wood's Colonial household gear was not adequate to furnish the mansion fully. Accordingly, pursuant to their plan, Huntoon donated his own collection to the Naomi Wood Estate. In the 1930's he wrote that his gift "comprises the greater part of the furniture now on display at Woodford Mansion" and that it was made in order to bring about "a complete Colonial Home, decorated and furnished in the proper style embracing natural domestic changes."[8] This action was picked up in the newspapers which reported his gift "of many of the pieces from his own famous collection."[9]

It was expected, said the press, that Woodford would be opened in the Fall of 1929. The estimate was close. Both the private reception on April 11, 1930, and the public opening on April 15 of the mansion refurnished "largely from the collections of Miss Wood and Mr. Huntoon," were duly reported.[10]

Moving the Park Guard out of Woodford was no simple matter. Transfer of their headquarters to the vacant Carousel building, a circular structure lying just within the West Park near the Belmont Avenue entrance, had been made, but the stables remained a problem. In 1930 it was reported to the Commission

---

By her Will Miss Naomi Wood directed her Trustees, Daniel T. V. Huntoon and the Girard Trust Company, to secure a house and furnish and maintain it "as an illustration of household gear during Colonial Years."

Through the courtesy of the Commissioners of Fairmount Park the Trustees have been enabled to occupy "Woodford," a mansion built in the middle of the Eighteenth Century and situated in the Park near the Thirty-third and Dauphin Streets entrance. It is itself a fine example of Colonial architecture, where has been installed the collection contemplated by Miss Wood, to which additions will be made from time to time and which will be open to the inspection of the public on stated days.

Prior to the inauguration of these days Mr. Huntoon and the Girard Trust Company hope that the Commissioners of Fairmount Park and the Managers of the Girard Trust Company will care to inspect "Woodford" and its contents, and they beg the pleasure of Mr.   's company at the Mansion on the afternoon of Thursday, April 11th, at four o'clock.

Philadelphia, March 31, 1930.

Printed invitation to private opening of The Naomi Wood Collection

that the guards themselves had finally "removed from Woodford Stable to the little tenant house nearby, and our forces are engaged in removing the modern sheds from around the old stable." One of the Mount Pleasant Mansion outbuildings was now used as the guards' stable and another was turned over to the "section foreman who formerly made his headquarters at Woodford Stables." The old stable or "chair house," freed of Park usage, was given repairs to roof and woodwork and painted.[11]

The exhibition elicited great enthusiasm from the public papers. The house and its new furnishings were carefully considered. It was reported that the Coleman period of occupancy "is still signified by the architecture." A matter of admiration were the "great fireplaces in every room."[12] The *New York Times* found that from its use as a police station when last seen, "now it is as fine an example of an 18th century mansion all ready to be lived in as there is in the country . . . The house's charm lies chiefly in the feeling of livableness that has been achieved, and the visitor has the feeling that he has stepped into a home from which the family is temporarily absent and to which it may return at any time to take up its daily round. This is a rare accomplishment in restoration and proves that Mr. Huntoon is an artist."[13] Here an important point was made, for it is this same quality which has then and through the subsequent years impressed both writers and visitors.

In 1931, with its move from Woodford completed, the Park improved the area surrounding the house, grading the site and planting trees and shrubs.[14] Driveway access to the mansion was

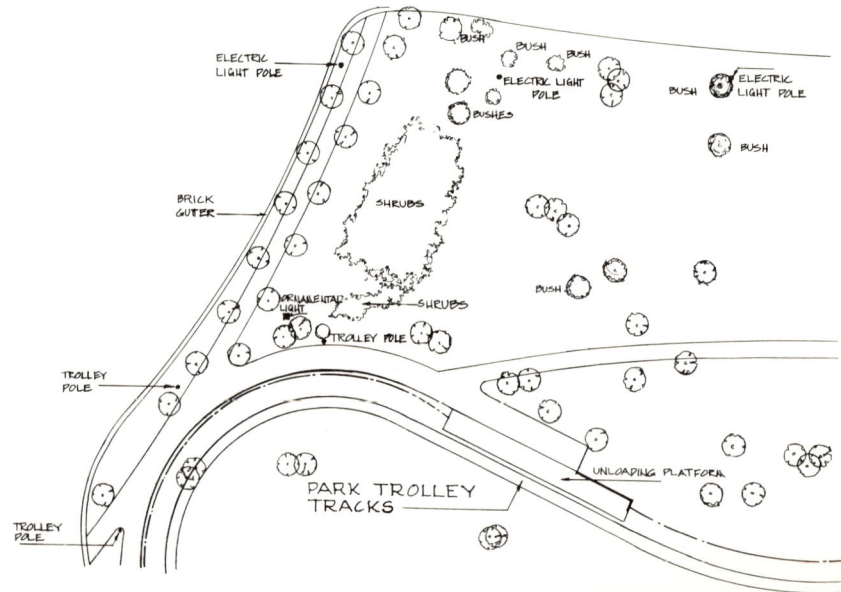

still limited to the rear because of the location of the trolley terminal,[15] and entrance by visitors was usually made from a small porch, newly constructed as part of the restoration, into the rear of the center hall which today is entered by the front door.

To celebrate the George Washington Bicentennial in 1932, the Associate Committee of Women of the Pennsylvania Museum of Art sponsored a pageant and house-showing of the restored Park mansions, in which Woodford and the Naomi Wood Collection participated. This was the first joint activity since the chain of houses was opened to the public a year earlier.[16]

Mr. Huntoon began purchasing and selling even before completion of the restoration in order to enlarge and upgrade the Collection as directed by the will. In 1929 he found the cream ware tea set now exhibited in the parlor. In 1931 he bought from the Art Museum the brass chandelier, and in 1932 the sconces, which now appear there. From the Metropolitan Museum of Art came in 1937 the pipe box now displayed in the dining room. Firearms, brass, silver and pewter objects were brought in. The acquisitions extended over twelve years, until the close of 1941.[17]

A picture of Mr. Huntoon's life at Woodford emerges from available sources.[18] He had been one of a group of bachelor "permanents" at the William Penn Inn in Gwynedd, a Philadelphia-area town, where a Mrs. Yuthers long presided as landlady. When the inn closed, the group dispersed and Huntoon moved to a hotel. With the opening of Woodford, Mrs. Yuthers returned to preside there as housekeeper and assisted in every phase of the running of the house. A maid kept the mansion and

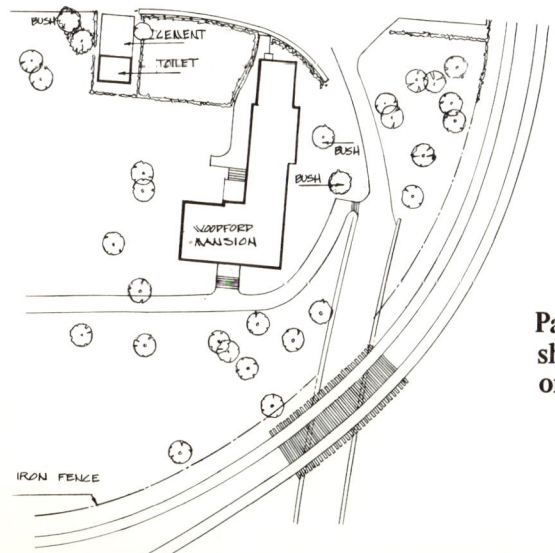

Park Commission plan ca. 1930 showing Park Trolley layout on Woodford front lawn

the Collection ready for visitors. A cook prepared meals. Lastly, Charles Hahn reported to the mansion daily as doorman and guide.

Huntoon was delighted with the privacy, independence and comfort Woodford provided. He was a reserved and quiet man with a good sense of humor—essentially a homebody who enjoyed reading, studying and welcoming friends, especially young people. Fond of dogs and horses, he had his small Scotch terrier, Wisp, at Woodford and he rarely missed a horse show in the Philadelphia suburbs. Oscar Seeley, a friend from the William Penn Inn days, was now a Paoli resident. Although Huntoon never drove an automobile, he was usually fetched on weekends by the Seeleys or their friends and driven to their home. Joseph Downs of the Museum of Art became his close friend.

Daniel Huntoon's primary interest was American furniture. He spent his vacations in New England, where it is said he was familiar with nearly every old house and antique shop and inspected them at leisure. Sometimes he visited there his nephew, his deceased brother's son, whom he had adopted. On these trips Mr. Huntoon was keen in his pursuit of old silver. In his last few years he was prevailed upon to make prolonged visits to his closest friend's summer home on the Maine coast. Although he had traveled somewhat in the South and West of the United States, he did not care for the ocean and never went abroad.

By 1940 Huntoon was coming to the end of his energies and began to put his affairs and the estate's in order. In June, 1939 he prepared an inventory of his own property on the premises of Woodford. Then came a "List of old silver in Woodford dining room." He prepared from the original bills of purchase a list of the estimated age of the objects on display at the mansion, as well as other memoranda including a listing of his purchases of silver and other household objects made for the estate through 1941 and a list of items sold on its behalf through 1939. Mr. Huntoon died January 15, 1943, leaving a house and exhibition the subject of superlatives in two articles in *Good Housekeeping*. After lengthy descriptions of the furnishings in the various rooms, the first concluded that "In its simple elegance and informal dignity Woodford exemplifies the ideal American house, whether old or new." The other described the furnished house as having "one of the handsomest Colonial living rooms in America, a number of beautiful mantels, and exquisite woodwork throughout."[19] Mr. Huntoon had faithfully, generously and assiduously carried out the responsibilities placed upon him. His portrait hangs at Woodford today.

Two weeks before his death Mr. Huntoon performed his last service for the estate, stemming from the fact that Miss Wood's will contained an interesting provision as to the succession of the individual trustees functioning in her perpetual trust. This was that each individual, beginning with Mr. Huntoon, should by his will select his successor—the corporate trustee remaining constant. In a codicil Mr. Huntoon named Mr. Sinkler to serve.[20] Sinkler had kept in touch with Mr. Huntoon and thus knew the Collection as well as the structure of Woodford.

In Mr. Huntoon's years the Collection had been displayed

A. C. Huntoon on Woodford steps with "Wisp"

largely on an informal basis. Much of his time was consumed in making the choice of items to be displayed, arranging and rearranging the exhibition, selecting and installing the proper curtains and furniture coverings. He is said to have remarked that he dreaded the day when the last detail would be accomplished. But it had been done. Now more time could be devoted to encouraging visits by the public.

One of Mr. Sinkler's first projects[21] was to research for and publish a booklet picturing each of the rooms at Woodford as furnished with the Collection, together with short descriptions and an introduction. He corresponded with members of Miss Wood's family and drew up genealogical charts. He reviewed materials respecting Mr. Huntoon and learned his background from his closest friends, the Talbot Aldriches of Boston. The first printing of the booklet occurred in 1947.[22] Four later printings followed for the purpose of reflecting in their photographs further acquisitions Sinkler made for the Collection. These included rugs, portraits and chairs, plus a primitive oil painting of Woodford Mansion labeled on the reverse "Woodford 1799" in an antique hand. He also made sales of furniture and books.

Mr. Sinkler was a man of decided tastes who required his custodian at Woodford to keep each piece of furniture and each decorative object exactly in the position he specified. Although he had studied at the Ecole des Beaux Arts in Paris, and although he had installed in Philadelphia the woodwork of a French chateau which he shipped home for the interior of a fine house, architecturally he leaned primarily toward Colonial American design. He was fastidious but very warm and gentle. For special visitors Mrs. Kabisch, the Woodford housekeeper, at his direction baked her oatmeal cookies which left the old kitchen with the aroma of spice to stimulate a friendly talk.

His love for the Collection shone through. His look upon the arrangement of it was ever fresh. He would become excited as he described a piece, and was flushed with victory at obtaining the Windsor chairs and the Wayne chairs at auction. "Jack" Sinkler, for so he preferred to be called, was the epitome of a late Victorian gentleman. Even his seldom-used swear words were voiced in his usual quiet and precise tone.

His wife, the former Mary Gadsden of Charleston, South Carolina, had exquisite taste and shared his love for the Collec-

John P. B. Sinkler Trustee, 1943 - 1959

tion. During the years of his connection with the estate as restorer of the mansion and trustee they lived in Chestnut Hill, within the city, with their three children. She predeceased him, and he died on February 10, 1959 at the age of eighty-four.

Exercising the privilege given him by Miss Wood's will, as early as 1944 Mr. Sinkler had written to Saipan to inquire of then naval Lieutenant Martin P. Snyder, who had already been introduced to the Trust and to Woodford, whether he would undertake the individual trusteeship at Sinkler's death. Thus came about[23] the present individual co-trustee's tenure in the position—the longest to date, extending from early 1959 for twenty-two years.

Martin Snyder, a practicing corporate and business lawyer and partner in the law firm of Morgan, Lewis and Bockius, and his wife, June Avery Snyder, were qualified in the historical, the aesthetic, and the business aspects of the trusteeship. He had already served as Historian for Old St. David's Church and Chairman of the Furnishing Committee at Pennsbury Manor, the restoration of William Penn's home on the Delaware; and was to become a Board member of the Historical Society of Pennsylvania, Moore College of Art and the Pennsylvania Academy of the Fine Arts, and a Commissioner of Valley Forge Park. She had served on the Board of the Print Club of Philadelphia and as Arts Chairman of the Board of the Philadelphia Junior League; and had first hand knowledge of the Park as a Director of Strawberry Mansion and of the annual Symposiums on Pennsylvania Gardens held in the Park 1955-1965, as well as Treasurer of the Colonial Dames of America who occupied Wakefield Mansion and later Lemon Hill. She was to become a member of the Philadelphia Committee for the American Museum in Bath, England and for many years was a Spring Guide at Winterthur Museum in Delaware. They have also served on numerous other public-service boards. Both have written and published extensively; and they have shared the researching and writing of this volume. Over the years the Collection, Woodford and their ramifying responsibilities have become a major effort in their lives, her role being that of a volunteer operating the museum.

Beginning in 1959 professional and amateur experts were invited to examine the Collection. This has continued through the years with the best in their fields on both sides of the ocean counseling upon it, sharing their knowledge and becoming its friends.

A brochure was published for distribution to visitors. Trips to house museums in Charleston, Annapolis, Boston and other centers of the east coast resulted in arrangements to distribute each other's pamphlets to increase visitation. The brochure[24] has been in use since 1959, with appropriate updates in the text.

The trustees planned and held a reception at Woodford in 1960 to celebrate the thirtieth anniversary of the opening of the Naomi Wood Collection to the public.[25] In that same year the Associate Committee of Women of the Philadelphia Museum of Art began guided tours of the Park mansions, including Woodford. These operated at first from hotels in center city[26] and in later years from the new City Visitors' Center, making the Park much more accessible to the public.

During these early years worn coverings and curtains were replaced with newly-selected fabrics. The mansion itself was repaired and strengthened, the working kitchen modernized, orientation receptions given, articles written and published, antiques studied and purchased, and the Museum of Art's Park House Guides trained in the Collection.

At the same time an investigation was begun of how to best restore a front driveway entrance to Woodford, which had been without one since operation of the Park railway at the mansion began in 1897. In 1962 Woodford's new driveway was installed by the city, after research into old maps and records, retention of experts, work on plans for drives, walks and plantings, and meetings with Fairmount Park and city representatives.

In 1963 a new front walk of old brick was laid and a generous gift received of forty boxwood bushes to line it. The mansion had now taken on its present front approach but remained unfenced. In the same year the West Chester Garden Club planted and maintained ground cover supplied by the Park nurseries, in preparation for the Garden Club of America's Fiftieth Anniversary Meeting in Philadelphia.

The University Hospital Antiques Show exhibited the Jacob Wayne armchair in 1964.[27] In the next year the first acquisitions of interesting pieces of delftware, ceramics appropriate to the furniture, were made. Much of it was found on family holidays abroad, one piece at a time. English experts lent their knowledge as their American counterparts had. The delftware, with its colorful accents, has engendered much interest in the Collection.

In 1971 Charles E. Peterson was retained to examine the three buildings comprising Woodford and give his opinion on the time of construction of the stable and the servants' house.[28] A year later the Naomi Wood Trust gave the pre-opening press reception at Woodford to inaugurate the "Colonial Style Christmas" tours of the Fairmount Park mansions, a project sponsored by the Park House Guides of the Philadelphia Museum of Art. These special days to see the mansions decorated for Christmas by local garden clubs have become an annual event bringing thousands to Fairmount Park during the first weekend in December. The December, 1978 issue of *Woman's Day* carried a picture story of Christmas at Woodford the previous year, which appeared one week before the annual tour. A long winding queue three abreast that was waiting when the front door opened, continued all day long. That afternoon a Channel 6 news truck passed. The photographer presented himself at the door with the comment "There must be a story here," and the Collection made its debut on prime time in the television newscasts that night.

Bicentennial endeavors commenced two years early, in 1974, with the use of Woodford for shooting scenes for the film "Twice

Upon A Congress," shown during the commemoration at the restored Bank of the United States in the city. The mansion was also the background for a part of a documentary film on Benjamin Franklin with Hugh Downs narrating.

The City of Philadelphia apportioned monies for the improvement of the Fairmount Park mansions for the Bicentennial visitors. Those allocated for Woodford went in part to replace the fencing at roof level and to fence the grounds for the first time since their purchase by the city. This last added both to Woodford's appearance and to its security. But the major restoration was of the servants' house, leaving the stable in need of similar assistance.

In 1975 a fire and theft security system in both the mansion and the servants' house with outdoor night lights, was installed by the Trust; preparatory personnel changes were made to handle the crowds; and arrangements were completed to meet the request for a loan from the Collection of one of the early Windsor comb-back chairs to the Philadelphia Museum of Art's Bicentennial exhibition. A separate corps of thirty-five volunteers for Woodford was trained. Complete inventories and descriptions of the items in the Collection were prepared for each exhibition room and retained there. A training manual was written for the guides. Authorities came—and still continue to come—to lecture to them on different facets of the Collection.

The Collection which presented itself for the celebration of two hundred years of American Independence had been pared down in nineteenth century items to more truly be "Colonial household gear."

With the translation of the guides' descriptions into seven languages and the production of easy-to-read charts identifying the origin of the delftware (with help from Michael Archer, Keeper of Ceramics at the Victoria and Albert Museum of London), Woodford was ready for the Bicentennial. The opening of the season saw the advent of Fairmount Park's picturesque "trolley-busses," previewed early in 1975, which made circular tours to the Park mansions from the center-city Visitors' Center. It was at this time also that the hours of visitation to Woodford and other mansions were unified and increased to a full day, six days each week.

During the past decade the Trust has worked closely with the

**Old Kitchen
Christmas 1977**

Fairmount Park Commission and Park personnel. The Park has initiated Spring "openings" of the trolley-bus tours serving eight Historic Mansions, including Woodford, and has provided basic guard services. The relationship has been warm, and helpful on both sides.

Public relations activities have steadily increased. In 1959, Woodford joined the National Trust for Historic Preservation. An article on the Collection was prepared and published in its national magazine. Another article was written for the November, 1962 issue of *Antiques Magazine*,[29] specially devoted to the Fairmount Park mansions. Since those early days many lectures and articles by each of husband and wife have emphasized varying aspects, from a short biography of Rebecca Franks to experiences as a guide, museum housekeeping and the installation of new personnel in the museum and their responsibilities.[30]

When the restored and modernized servants' house became available, a new type of arrangement was concluded with young custodians in both that house and the mansion whereby services were received in return for occupancy of the quarters. This has continued to the present.

With the quickening of pace in all phases of the Trust, the energies of two individuals in supervising the operation of the mansion have been utilized. Mrs. Snyder has for years functioned daily, supervising the museum in matters as wide-ranging as training and scheduling personnel; maintenance problems; relationships with the Park, with other mansions, with the city and the media; special tours visiting the Collection. She has produced an initial catalog of it, shared in the decisions for all acquisitions, and conducted needlework sessions where Woodford's guides produced the curtains hanging in the stairhall and the old kitchen, following drawings by the Trust's interior decorations advisor W. Stanleigh Krewson. She is directly responsible for the way in which both the Collection and the mansion present themselves to visitors.

On April 15, 1980, the Naomi Wood Collection at Woodford Mansion attained fifty years of being open to the public. The cover of the May issue of the *Antique Collector* published in London announced "American Collection's Fiftieth Anniversary"—and in an article by June Avery Snyder, Woodford and its Collection became the first American house to be included in its "Open To The Public" series of six houses each year.[31] Each such English house must be still lived in by a descendant of the original owner.

On May 16, 1980, just a month after the fiftieth anniversary, the United States Department of the Interior awarded a plaque designating Woodford a National Historic Landmark at ceremonies in the Mayor's reception room. The plaque bears the date 1978—the year when such status was in fact conferred. The mansion also carries the Historic Landmarker of the city's Historical Commission.

The Park House Guides and the newly-formed organization of eight "Fairmount Park Historic Mansions" also celebrated with a reception at Woodford "The Naomi Wood Collection's Golden Anniversary at Woodford Mansion."

Dining Room
Christmas, 1979

The outlook for the future is one of increasing service. Every effort is made to bring home to the visitor the sturdy and self-reliant way of life of our predecessors and to make those qualities desirable in today's more complex and fast-moving society. Many visitors, by no means all of them American, are examining the American approach to particular questions important to them. They realize that their ancestors were in various ways freer than they themselves are now. They see that one who stands up and is counted can help change his world—it worked two hundred years ago. A remark by a visitor that "People believed in ideals then," prompted another in the large group to speak up, "A lot of us still do." Some express indignation that a few are trying to turn the American dream into a nightmare by force and terror. Visitors are reassuring in their curiosity, vitality and enthusiasm for our country; and the Collection stirs positive chords. Increasingly, too, visitors are repeaters who appreciate the quality of the Collection in their individual fields of interest. The combined Collection and house often serve as a study museum.

Behind it all, Miss Wood has been the catalyst. The trustees, the staff and the guides encourage our visitors, in the words of T. S. Eliot, to "take heart for the future, remembering the past."

Martin P. Snyder

Naomi Wood at age 16 (1887)

The Naomi Wood Collection Today

The Collection represents the input from four different sources. The objects left by Miss Wood under her will form the first. Mr. Huntoon's gift of his own collection forms a large and important second segment. A third consists of purchases made by Mr. Huntoon as the first trustee with funds from the newly-established Naomi Wood Trust in order to augment the basic pieces with smaller homelike furnishings. Lastly, following Miss Wood's will, there are the acquisitions made by the two succeeding trustees to augment the Collection.

The objects in it were not originally at Woodford but are furnishings that (with few exceptions) could have been there in the period of the Barclays and the Franks. Various similar pieces are listed in the Barclay inventory of property there; and David Franks' collection of books was sold at auction just before his exile to New York.

NAOMI WOOD
COLLECTION
Front Hall

NAOMI WOOD COLLECTION
Parlor

NAOMI WOOD COLLECTION
Parlor

NAOMI WOOD COLLECTION
Dining Room

NAOMI WOOD COLLECTION
Dining Room

NAOMI WOOD
COLLECTION
Old Kitchen

NAOMI WOOD COLLECTION
Old Kitchen

NAOMI WOOD
COLLECTION

Nursery

Rebecca Franks,
Lady Johnson

Sir Henry Johnson

NAOMI WOOD COLLECTION
Upper Front Hall

NAOMI WOOD COLLECTION

Upper Front Hall

NAOMI WOOD
COLLECTION
Maple Room

NAOMI WOOD COLLECTION
Maple Room

NAOMI WOOD COLLECTION
Bedroom

NAOMI WOOD COLLECTION
Bedroom

NAOMI WOOD COLLECTION
Bedroom

Upon stepping into Woodford through the high and heavy front doors with their small glass panes, you walk back in time into the elegant Georgian world of candlelight and fireplace heat of the eighteenth century. You find yourself in the center hall extending from front to back of the original one-story structure. This was a room, not just a "passage." You might have stopped simply to leave a note in the hanging letter box.[1] If you have come to pay a call, you would leave your riding crop in one of the large Italian pottery jars and rinse your hands in the Chinese porcelain basin with rose water from the matching bottle below. Powder for powdering your wig is in a drawer of the basin stand.

The tall glass wind shade on the Philadelphia Chippendale block-footed card table protects its candle from drafts of air. The scissor-type snuffer alongside both trims the wick and snuffs the flame. The Chippendale looking glass reflects and increases the candlelight. The cherry candlestand with its sliding candle drawer lights the wide front of the hall.

You might sit upon one of the two Philadelphia side chairs which are part of a set of six (they belonged to the Wharton family). Their obvious quality, the simple beauty of their proportions without carving details, and their solidity, all bespeak their Quaker origin. You note the appealing small portraits which tell you at once of the emphasis on family continuity.*

You now enter the parlor—architecturally formal, yet in size so comfortable for family living—which faces south and is lighted by five tall windows. The ceiling is high as befits such a room, but the pleasing curved coving permits a feeling of intimacy in the whole.

The tone of the room is set by the carved, broken-pediment overmantel and its restful landscape scene. A fine Chinese export porcelain garniture of five pieces in famille rose, the flowing brass finials of the andirons and the brass-handled fire tools from Woodford's early days, complete this salient feature.

The parlor furniture, pre-Revolutionary, in the Chippendale style, is of the finest Philadelphia craftsmanship, and matches the overmantel in elegance. The camelback mahogany sofa and footstools and the slant-top desk balance the weight of the fireplace and overmantel. A graceful tea table, with fine carved knees, is

---

*(The modern portrait of Daniel T. V. Huntoon, while an anachronism, honors Naomi Wood's first trustee and in this respect shares the hall with the bronze plaque attesting to National Historic Landmark status.)

drawn to the center of the room and set with Leedsware and silver, ready for use. The solid-splat arm chair and various shell-carved side chairs are of walnut as is the early commode roundabout chair that stands beside an English writing desk.

A rare four-armed English chandelier acquired from the Philadelphia Museum of Art's Charles F. Williams Collection, gilt bronze sconces from the Duke of Leeds' Hornby Castle, Yorkshire, England (dismantled about 1931), and candlesticks of brass in varying styles, serve to illuminate the eighteenth century portraits. Books of the period are ready at hand to be read at the desk or in the mahogany wing chair. The coconut cup, silver-mounted, initialed and dated, is a wedding present, brought back from the new trade extending to the Pacific.

The blue of the damask draperies and of the sofa is echoed in the fine Kerman rug and lends a predominant feeling of coolness to this sunny room, countered by the many brass accents.

You cross to the dining room. Hepplewhite was the fashionable style for a separate room for that purpose, which came into vogue, in fine houses, soon after the Revolution. The furnishings revolve around a New England mahogany dining table of adjustable length, the half-moon ends of which could readily be used separately. The lighter feeling of the new furniture style is manifested in the tapering legs and the use of inlays of lighter color. The "shield back" chairs are of two related American styles and sources. One arm chair and three side chairs were made in Philadelphia by Jacob Wayne, cousin of "Mad Anthony" Wayne of Revolutionary fame (the Collection has a copy of the bill of sale) and are carved in a wheat sheaf pattern. The remaining five chairs, of New England "Salem" design, blending well with those of local origin, belonged to the Reverend Benjamin Huntoon, Mr. Huntoon's grandfather.

The graceful American mahogany sideboard and its knife boxes are surmounted by a gilt-framed, American-eagle girondole looking glass. Both American and English silversmiths (including three generations of Hester Bateman's family) are represented in the sideboard display.

The mahogany butler's secretary at which he kept his records, in the opposite corner, is a Philadelphia piece, again inlaid. The inlaid clock upon it is the work of Abner Jones of Weare, New Hampshire, dated 1786. It has a unique strike. Handsome tall hurricane candlesticks of English Sheffield with their original glass chimneys, stand upon the secretary along with decanters and tea caddies shaped as fruit.

A Chinese export tureen in famille rose, on the card table between the windows, reminds you that porcelain was replacing the earlier-favored handpainted English delftware pottery seen in rare forms and decorations in the closets and in place settings on the table. A large export hunt bowl in the center of the table and a covered sweetmeat dish are also "in the latest fashion."

Above the fireplace hang a pair of Waterford sconces. Portraits of James Searles Woodward and Sarah Richardson Waln, both of Philadelphia, share the walls with rare polychrome Pennsylvania German pottery plaques of George III and Queen Charlotte and a pair of oil paintings of fowl by Peter Holstein (1580-1662).

Small brass ember tongs hang by the fireplace, ready to remove a coal to light the pipes kept in the Pennsylvania pipe and tobacco box, inlaid with the American Eagle. Beneath it stands a mahogany chest-on-frame containing its full complement of a dozen olive-green, hand-blown bottles for spirits.

Warmth is lent to this north room not only by colorful ceramics, but by draperies of gold-figured silk damask (woven by Scalamandré). The Persian rug is a Sarouk.

You note that the unique lower stair hall lying behind the dining room exhibits much earlier furniture styles. A walnut tall chest of Pennsylvania origin and a high-backed New England arm chair are of the William and Mary period; the two side tables are of the somewhat later Queen Anne style, one with scrolled apron on the front and sides. The hall is furnished as a way station to the second floor. At the foot of the stairs, the hanging lead-lined candle box holds fresh candles. On the table the brass "chambersticks" stand ready to light the way upward. A leather fire bucket, a reminder of the ever-present threat of fire, is a necessary adjunct. An English "bird cage" or "lantern" clock, made in London (1658) by Edward Norris at the symbol of Crossed Keys, hangs on the wall. A Chinese export punch bowl bears the arms of the Honourable Society of Bucks, an eighteenth century English patriotic organization.

In the upper stair hall you again find Pennsylvania pieces—a blanket chest and a tall case clock—both of walnut and both conveniently placed for family needs. The bonnet of the clock betrays its early style, as does its full brass face inscribed with the name of Benjamin Morris. George Washington, a Mason, is on the wall. A masonic ballot box below, used for voting by dropping a concealed white or black ball into the open end, made a defeating black ball anonymous. An Artillery Captain's gold-braided epaulets rest in a handsome epaulet box of inlaid walnut. The samplers were made by ancestors of Naomi Wood. A Persian Mosoul rug lies underfoot.

Turning into the nursery, you can readily visualize a nursemaid daydreaming on the unusual early English caned day-bed from the Williams Collection, while children play on the floor or do sums at the small American desk-on-frame. The top of the bureau for their clothing extends backwards flush with the wall. It is locally made of mahogany as is the mirror above it. An unusual single-drawer sewing box (nineteenth century) on the primitive oak candlestand combines a pin cushion top with a different hole, trimmed with ivory, for each color thread. Five fabric animals from New England, whose delightful "pin feathers" are the protruding heads of old pins, stride the the mantel of the corner fireplace. They are joined by a wooden bird carved by Schimmel of Lancaster in the nineteenth century. A Pennsylvania German rocking horse is near the hearth. The small doll has a paper maché head, kid body and wooden legs.

You note that each end of the upper front hall boasts a pair of the Wharton side chairs. Under the Palladian window, between one pair, stands an important Philadelphia Chippendale dressing table made on order for Jonathon Leedham as a wedding present. On this "lowboy" an early, steep-sided polychrome bowl of English delftware is flanked by a pair of brass candlesticks on molded octagonal bases.

At the back of the hall the chairs sit close to a Philadelphia birdcage tea table for tea upstairs. Here the Tory occupancy of Woodford at the time of the Revolution is most felt. Admiral Howe, who opened the Delaware for British supplies, and Marquis Cornwallis, who took possession of Philadelphia, appear in engravings. A Bristol delftware bowl with its inner inscription "Success to British Arms by Sea & Land" sits at one end of the great Philadelphia Chippendale block-footed sofa. Above it the large color print (nineteenth century) of Benjamin Franklin at the

Court of France is a somewhat incongruous reminder that the Doctor was a frequent visitor to Woodford. An early Pennsylvania gateleg table can be opened for various uses.

To the left of this airy upper hall, with its soft Caucasian rugs underfoot, you enter the bedroom overlooking the entranceway into Woodford. Its curtains and bedhangings carry forward the same feeling. The Chippendale block-footed cherry bed was made in Philadelphia or nearby. A local overstuffed chair of the same style sits near its foot, beside a window sill supporting a soothing nineteenth-century wind harp. This is the chair that an expert on early American furniture circled years ago, saying aloud, "The chair should be English. Most of these chairs were English. But it looks American to me. If it is beech, it is English but something about it just *smells* American." Later, an analysis of the wood proved him right.

The William and Mary dressing table, stool and looking glass, and the Jacobean side chair, could have belonged to an earlier generation of the family. The Hepplewhite corner washstand holding a Chinese export basin and water bottle are of later date.

The glory of the room is the William and Mary high chest of drawers, purchased by Naomi Wood from Wallace Nutting who dated it 1700-1710. It is pictured in his book *Furniture of the Pilgrim Century*[2] and was exhibited in the ground-breaking Girl Scout Antique Show in New York in 1923.

Over the mantel hangs an early eighteenth-century American portrait of four-year-old Amelia Van Overbeck of the Hudson Valley. It shows her family's coat of arms. The close pair of polychrome Fazackerly delftware wall pockets above the fireplace are from the Garner Collection. Among the ivory miniatures displayed is one of a British officer in his red coat. Two ivory boxes, one still containing face patches, and a long-handled ivory hand used to reach under wigs as a scalp scratcher, share the dressing table with a tiny seventeenth-century delftware ointment jar made in Lambeth, south of London.

You cross to the maple room, which matches the downstairs parlor in position on the south side but is much more informal in its atmosphere. Here, in what was originally two bedrooms, Naomi Wood looks from over the fireplace on furniture which is mostly of American maple and contains much that is unusual.

A New England tall case clock, two American wing chairs for

comfort while playing games, early Spanish-footed New England chairs, and a dropleaf table with gaming board and carved ivory pieces, invite relaxation. A long clay pipe, tobacco box and brass tamper are close at hand. Books, a terrestrial globe and a solitaire board with Bristol glass marbles all contribute to the feeling of quiet enjoyment.

Beside a game of loo, one of the few surviving sets of the British newspaper, The *Pennsylvania Ledger,* published in Philadelphia during the occupation (1777-1778), lies open to the description of the Mischianza Ball given to General Howe at his departure—a triumphant night for beautiful Rebecca Franks.

A New England maple desk-on-frame displays a taper jack used to melt sealing wax, a maple seal box, a brass seal with maple handle, a wick pick and a candle snuffer—all important for the family's correspondence. A maple telescope rests on a sill.

The maple-paneled settee, said to be of Canadian origin, stands before colorful chintz curtains and behind a mellow Ferreghan rug.

You return downstairs to one of the most interesting rooms at Woodford, the old kitchen. Its focal point, the fireplace, is still furnished with a crane enabling pots or kettles to be swung to and from the main fire, as well as out over the broad hearth on which small fires were laid under three-legged pots. The mantel shelf holds an acorn clock (nineteenth century) from Connecticut with a no-nonsense strike. Kitchen tools and lighting implements are ready at hand.

The early Pennsylvania walnut gateleg table is surrounded by an excellent collection of Windsor chairs from the J. Stogdell Stokes Collection. One of these, displaying knuckled arms, was a part of the Philadelphia Museum of Art's Bicentennial exhibition "Philadelphia: Three Centuries of American Art" and is illustrated and described in that catalog.[3] It, or possibly an identical chair, appears in Nutting's *Furniture Treasury.*[4]

The pewter and delftware collections are both represented on the table. One of the handsome tankards is the work of an outstanding eighteenth-century pewterer, the Revolutionary officer Colonel William Will of Philadelphia. Many unusual shapes of pewter abound, from a tab-handled American porringer made by Elisha Kirk in 1785 to a wine strainer used in decanting. Some rest upon a Delaware Valley ball-footed chest of drawers helpful for storage. Spoons are kept in their hanging rack.

A choice selection of polychrome English delftware brightens the entire room with its colorful birds and flowers—some marked to evidence earlier ownership in other collections. There can be found along with chargers and smaller plates, posset pots, and vessels for liquids including a wet drug jar. Among the few Dutch pieces are a pair of large tobacco jars made by William Van der Does and marked with the sign of the Three Bells manufactory at Delft. These stand atop an early Delaware Valley shoe-footed pine cupboard. The companion (English) dresser was removed from the Fountain House Tavern (1732) in Doylestown, Pennsylvania.

Two quite rare Chester County walnut side chairs of the early eighteenth century, a rush-seated New England round-about chair, Spanish-footed, of about the same age, a fireplace bench and a bench table provide ample seating for kitchen chores. The oil painting and the watercolor depicting Woodford hang here.

* * * *

The Naomi Wood Collection's strong illusion of being at home in a mansion of the stature of Woodford is due not only to the completeness of its "household gear," but equally to the cohesiveness and high quality of the furnishings as a whole—a factor consciously applied by each of the trustees. Sinkler secured the Jacob Wayne chairs in the dining room, the Windsor chairs, spoon rack and painting in the old kitchen, portraits, rugs and smaller articles. The present authors have acquired the Chinese export porcelain; the English delftware; the Wharton family chairs; the parlor table, rug and coconut cup; the highstyle Chippendale dressing table; the scrolled Queen Anne table in the stair hall; the two large kitchen dressers; the Chester County side chairs and the pewter tankards; the Tory newspaper run and the Tory corner; and the current curtains and furniture coverings. Generous gifts of furniture and rugs have enabled them to arrange a nursery, floor the maple room, and add examples to the old kitchen's hooked rugs. A fine silver mote spoon was given to the silver collection. Foundations have made possible the installation of air conditioning and the cleaning and restoration of portraits.

A strengthened Collection enters its second fifty years better carrying to the public the intangible values Naomi Wood wanted to bring to them.

XI
Architectural Development
of Woodford Mansion

From the start Woodford Mansion followed in its exquisite formality upon the principles of Georgian architecture then very popular in England and coming into use in the Colonies. These were largely derived from Palladio and the Renaissance which in turn had been inspired by classical sources. Woodford is held by architects to represent, along with Mount Pleasant Mansion, Cliveden, and the Powel House in center city, "the best domestic examples of the middle Georgian style in the Philadelphia area."[1]

One of the features of Georgian construction, probably due to the fire of London, was the use of brick. By this time brick was manufactured as a common structural article of good quality in Philadelphia. Although it has been said that Woodford's bricks were imported from England, this seems dubious.[2] The use of Flemish bond as the brick pattern for the original house was consistent with practice in Philadelphia of the period whereby in the best houses bricks laid lengthwise were alternated laterally with bricks laid end-on. This gave a pleasing effect but was more expensive than the usual brick courses. In the city Flemish bond was a feature of the front facade; here it covers the entire two-story structure. Black headers were used only on the northern wall of Woodford rather than in the front facade.

The first floor was raised in accordance with Georgian design, and was reached by six soapstone steps which remain today along with their iron railings. The steps led to a Doric, commonly called a "Tuscan" or "Roman" doorway, favored in Philadelphia Georgian architecture, which accentuated the formality of the house. With nine-foot doors lighted only by two small high-up quatrefoil windows, the massive effect of the mansion was emphasized. Engaged columns were added at the sides of the doorway to support its classical architrave and formal triangular pediment. Another feature was the addition as a part of the brick walls of decorative embryonic pilasters near each of the four corners and a similar forward projection of an entire area of the wall and woodwork surrounding the doorway, stressing its importance.

The roof was not pitched, but flat, yet it sloped at the sides as a hip roof, the remains of which can be seen today in the shape of an apparent pent-eave. These last were a common feature around Philadelphia,[3] used particularly by the Pennsylvania German settlers. The hip roof left a rectangular deck possibly bound by a wooden balustrade, reached by a trapdoor and used as a "captain's walk." This feature was "almost universal in the better homes of relatively square mass."[4]

With windows high for the period, panes twelve over twelve, and with more height than the first story, considered alone today, would indicate, because of the presence of a completely plastered attic or garret,[5] the exterior must have presented a handsome and affluent appearance in contrast with the farm houses which were then the only existing homes in the area.

Inside, the house equally well carried out Georgian principles. A handsome center hall was set off by two fluted pilasters connected by a Doric frieze, and by an unusual coved ceiling.[6] The principle of formal balance in the construction was followed by creating rooms on either side which utilized equal space. That on the south side was the parlor or drawing room, which was also deeply coved. With five windows, this was a beautifully sunny room. The entire fireplace wall was paneled, consistently with the practice of the style and period. The overmantel or chimney breast, with broken pediment embellished by a rococo cartouche, was handsomely carved in the style of Grinling-Gibbons and has always attracted great attention. One of the most recent books to treat of the fireplace has said that "Its beautifully carved overmantel, its coved ceiling, its marble surround, and its excellent proportions establish it as one of the finest in America."[7] It does not appear to have been copied from a particular plate in Swan's popular architectural books published in London; yet it seems in almost every detail to have been itself the source for plate XXVII of the *Articles and Rules* of the Carpenters' Company of Philadelphia published in 1786.[8]

The corresponding space on the north side was divided by a partition into two bedchambers. The first insurance survey, 1769, speaks of "newel stairs," presumably leading to the attic. In Georgian homes the stairway was commonly placed at one side of the rear of the hallway; but since at Woodford the attic was not space commonly in use and since there appears to be no trace in the existing hall of the removal of a stairway at a later date, it may be assumed that the stairway lay in the rear of the two bedchambers. Each of these, not coved, was fitted with a fireplace, apparently in a corner position,[9] and a simpler form of cornice and mantel.

The interior was completed by a kitchen in the cellar. Probably this was reached by a staircase lying below that leading from the first floor to the garret. No trace of such a stair appears, but portions of the construction beneath the first floor support the conclusion that the two corner fireplaces were in the same positions as those surviving in the corresponding rooms remaining today on the second floor.

Another fine feature of the interior lay in the random width doweled flooring, which according to the survey, made up "the greatest part of the floor." Each board was pinned in position by wooden dowels which still remain in place. This original flooring survives in the parlor.

There was no separate dining room. It was customary to eat wherever tables might be set up for the occasion as desired.[10]

Several twentieth-century authors have stated that the chimney contained a casting bearing the coat-of-arms of the owner and the date 1742. This led to the assertion that 1742 is the date of the original construction.[11] These statements are belied by the first fire insurance survey, which described the house as "about ten years old"; and by the fact that William Coleman did not purchase the land until 1756. One description of Woodford reports that "the iron date stone was carried by the Park Guards from the Robin Hood Tavern." Whatever its source, it can no longer be found.

The fireplace surround is said to have been decorated by tiles of delftware which were discarded in the restoration of 1928. This is another enigma. Two secondary sources go so far as to state that the tiles pictured Elizabethan knights and their ladies.[12] However, four blue and white delftware tiles have been framed and are preserved in the house today, bearing a notation by Mr. Huntoon that they are original tiles once used in the mansion. They bear well-known floral patterns of English eighteenth-century delftware tiles. The incomplete shop drawings now available fail to show substitution of the present marble surround for tiles in the restoration. Marble was the usual choice in Philadelphia Georgian of the 1750s;[13] it was readily obtainable from King of Prussia nearby.

Against such an elegant background handsome Philadelphia Chippendale furniture should have been installed. Yet there is no listing in the inventory of Coleman's estate of individual pieces of furniture in Woodford at his death. Its furnishings are listed only in a "lump" item at approximately twenty-eight pounds, while the value accorded by the inventory to the furniture in Coleman's town house at Second and Pine Streets was nine times as great.[14] Woodford was only a summer-months home.

It appears to have been built as a complex of three buildings beginning in 1756, the year when Coleman acquired the acreage, and completed in 1757. Surviving fragments of Coleman's account book[15] show small payments to Nicholas Hicks in January, 1758 "for Stone Work" and to Richard Lacock on February 1 for "Housebuilding for painting"—both probably relating to the two stone outbuildings, which would be built last, since the entries seem to be the last clearly relating to construction. One other at the end of the year covers a small payment for "Sundry jobs done in the Country," as does one in February, 1759, but like entries probably continued over the years. Some suggest that the four-room quarters for servants and the stable were already there and had been built by the Shutes in the 1730s or 1740s for farming use—furnishing a ready connection, by their nearness to the Wissahickon Road, with the city—one used for the housing of extra farm workers over the summer and Fall and the other for the housing of farm animals and implements. But it appears more likely that all three buildings were erected at the same time.[16] The small house and the stable were both constructed of stone; farm outbuildings in those days were usually wooden. The servants' house was built with a full cellar and a fireplace in each of its rooms on both floors—hardly the style for warm-season farm hands. The tilt of the original roof lines of all three buildings appears to have been the same, an angle lower than the usual roof slope of farm buildings. The two stone buildings are oriented to approximately the same compass point as the mansion; they are of identical size and are placed substantially equidistant from the main structure. The advertisement by the sheriff of the approaching sale at which Coleman bought the property made no mention of any structure on the acreage, but only "a piece or parcel of land."[17] Such advertisements touted any features which would add something more than mere land value to the price—particularly permanent buildings. Nor did the deed convey more than "a certain piece of land" and any rights pertaining to it.

A natural inquiry has been that of who was the builder retained to design and erect Woodford. Records are lacking, nor has any reference been found settling the question. It seems probable that the original one-story structure was the work of Samuel Rhoads or Robert Smith, Philadelphia's preeminent master builders or "house carpenters" as they were then known.[18] Woodford was built with that elegance and fineness of detail which was the mark of an experienced builder of homes of this type, one who would know and follow the details of construction utilized in England's Georgian structures copied here. Rhoads designed the Pennsylvania Hospital (1755) and was President for ten years preceding his death in 1784 of the Carpenters' Company of Philadelphia, builders of Carpenters' Hall. He was a good friend of Coleman and is said by Nicholas Wainwright "probably" to have erected Coleman's new town house ten years later, in 1766.[19] Coleman's "dear wife Hannah's" death toward the end of 1768 called forth a codicil dated December 13, signed in the presence of three witnesses, one of whom was Samuel Rhoads.

Smith was occupied until 1756 with Nassau Hall at Princeton and from 1758 to 1761 was in charge of the construction of St. Peter's Church; but he was apparently free for a commission such as Woodford in 1757. Both men were involved in building Franklin's house in 1764-1766.[20]

The first insurance survey was prepared after slight changes were made by Alexander Barclay in 1769. It shows that he added a "quite new" piazza or porch ten feet wide extending the whole length of the back of the house. This feature signaled the start of much living in the area of the garden facing the river. Since his son, Robert, had already been sent to London, Barclay had only his wife and daughter Patience at home and hence had no need to change the internal arrangement of the mansion. The insurance company's records show, however, that its coverage was approved only "When Iron Rails are put up on the Tenement."[21] This could only refer to the area of the roof.

Barclay's sister-in-law and her husband, Margaret and David Franks, who had several children at home, greatly enlarged the mansion when they purchased it, creating substantially the building seen today. The differences between the insurance survey of 1769 and the new one issued for Franks in November, 1772[22] show at once the nature of Franks' changes. Woodford became "2 Storys high" (plus an attic). A graceful and airy stairhall was added by building on to the rear of the old house on the northwest. Upstairs the new area over the parlor was divided into two rooms and two more were constructed over the ground-floor bedrooms. A new center hall over that downstairs terminated above the front entrance with a fine three-part Palladian window, much the style in the finer Georgian homes. An entirely new two-story wing extended back from, and on a level lower than, the new stairhall. This wing, the "backbuildings" of the survey, contained on the ground floor a large kitchen with cooking fireplace and, above, a similarly large room with north and south exposures, completely paneled on the fireplace wall. Traditionally this last room has been referred to as "the ballroom," but there is no record that it was so used. With the new kitchen in use, the old one in the cellar was abandoned.

The rear porch, only a few years old, had to be reduced in length by the bulk of the new extension cutting across it. It continued to have access to the front of the house by high doors at the rear of the original center hall, and was now reached as well from a new arched doorway at the side of the stairhall. This made an easy passage between the back of the house and the parlor.

The feature of a hip roof and balustrade was retained a full story above the level of the old ones. The slender wooden rails forming patterns in the panels were shaped in the Chinese Chippendale pattern then so popular.[23] Both the oil painting and the watercolor of Woodford show such a balustrade in place, as does a 1900 publication illustrating the front elevation of the house.[24]

Prominent modillioned eaves were installed at the new roofline. That portion of the original lower roof which protruded beyond the walls now marked the separation of the original one-story section from the upper story.

The outside aspect of Woodford became most interesting. The rear extension, a recognized Georgian form, created an appealing stepped-down side elevation. The front view became much more imposing than before with the addition of the divided window and above it a triangular modillioned roofline pediment somewhat larger in size than that which already crowned the front entrance. The facade was now embellished with the approach steps, the imposing doorway, the lower pediment, the Palladian window, and the roof pediment, one above the other.[25] Yet this strong vertical impression, supplemented by the relatively high windows, was countered by a heavy horizontal pent eave, the heavy modillioned upper eave and the rail of the balustrade to make an integrated and satisfying whole.

With all these changes Woodford became the roomy and substantial early Georgian structure which the Fairmount Park Commission concluded should remain standing in the Park even though other houses, including nearby Edgeley, were removed. This was fortunate, for the mansion has been characterized as "one of the most charming examples of Colonial architecture in America"[26] which, with its "simple, massive proportions is full of a quiet and peaceful dignity."[27] Its ground-breaking arched stairhall doorway[28] has recently been copied as one of the doors in the new (1980) American Wing of the Metropolitan Museum of Art.

Who, as a builder, added the new features? Here again, either Samuel Rhoads or Robert Smith. Rhoads had a close relationship with the Barclays for he had built Barclay's town house in the 1750s on a lot split off from his own. It was through the Barclays that the Franks knew Woodford.

Apparently Thomas Paschall did not alter the mansion; but in that case his successor, Isaac Wharton, made further changes to accommodate the stylistic demands of a new generation. He combined the two sleeping rooms on the ground floor and those on the south side of the second story in each case into one large room.

The corner fireplaces of the earlier rooms were discarded and in each "double" room one large fireplace and overmantel was installed in the new Federal style. This created a separate dining room downstairs, and upstairs a sunny bedroom facing south. No survey has been found which would date this work.

During the early 1800s Woodford received a coat of buff-colored paint over its brick exterior. Large areas of this on the south side remain today to give the house its unusual tawny color.

Lending support to the probability that the expanded grounds became a working farm under the Whartons is the increased number of outbuildings which began to spring up. When the property was deeded to the city as a part of Fairmount Park in 1869 there were at least six such structures occupying various positions at the rear of the property.[29] At perhaps the mid nineteenth century, the servants' house received a rear lean-to shed which expanded its working space. A new doorway was cut through the rear wall to enter it from the interior. It was probably now used by a tenant. The shed itself was later expanded and a Victorian front porch was also added before purchase by the Park.[30] Numerous extensions elongated the stable from its south wall; and even the mansion appears on the Park's initial survey plans to be extended at the rear by a shed. Such a shed appears in

Measured drawings of the Woodford structure

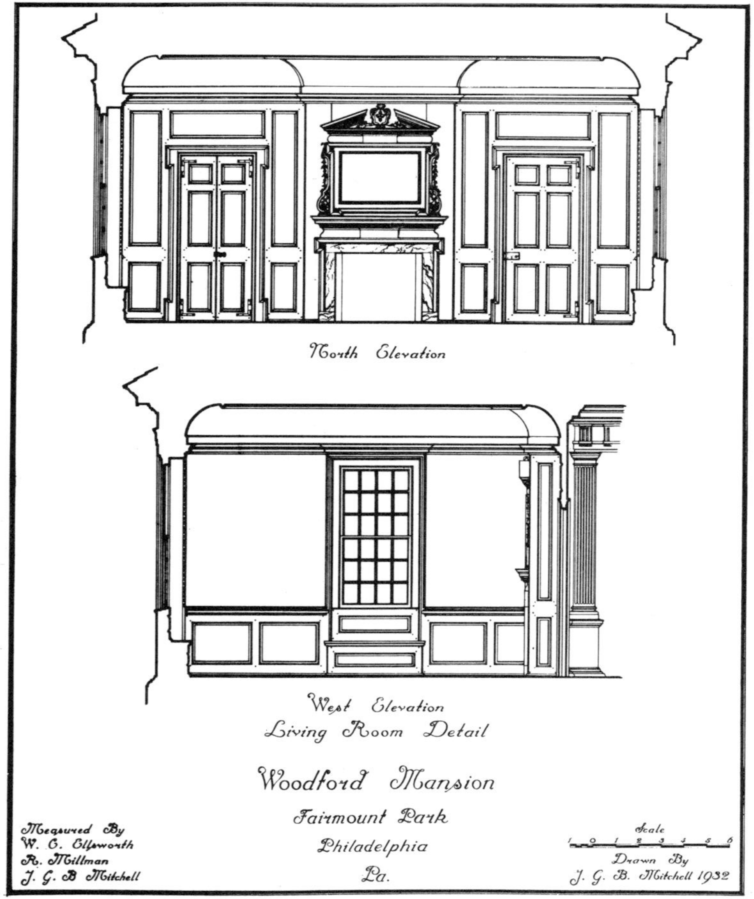

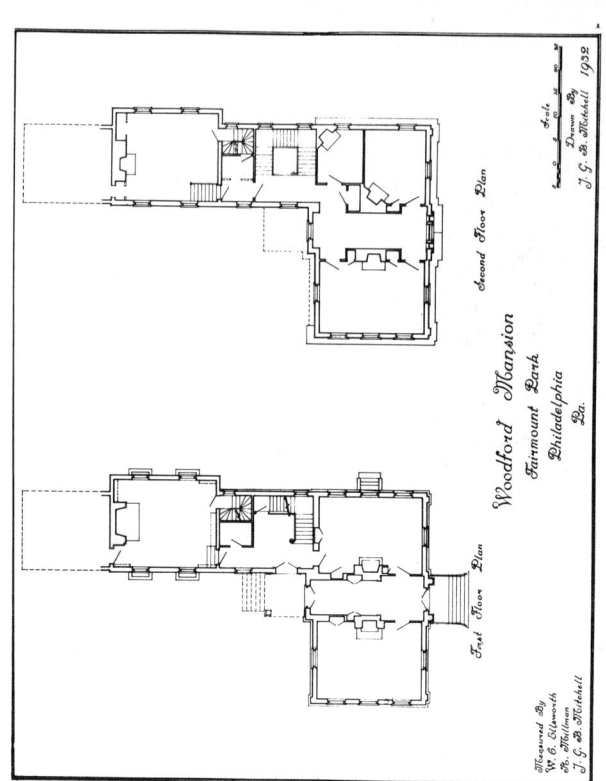

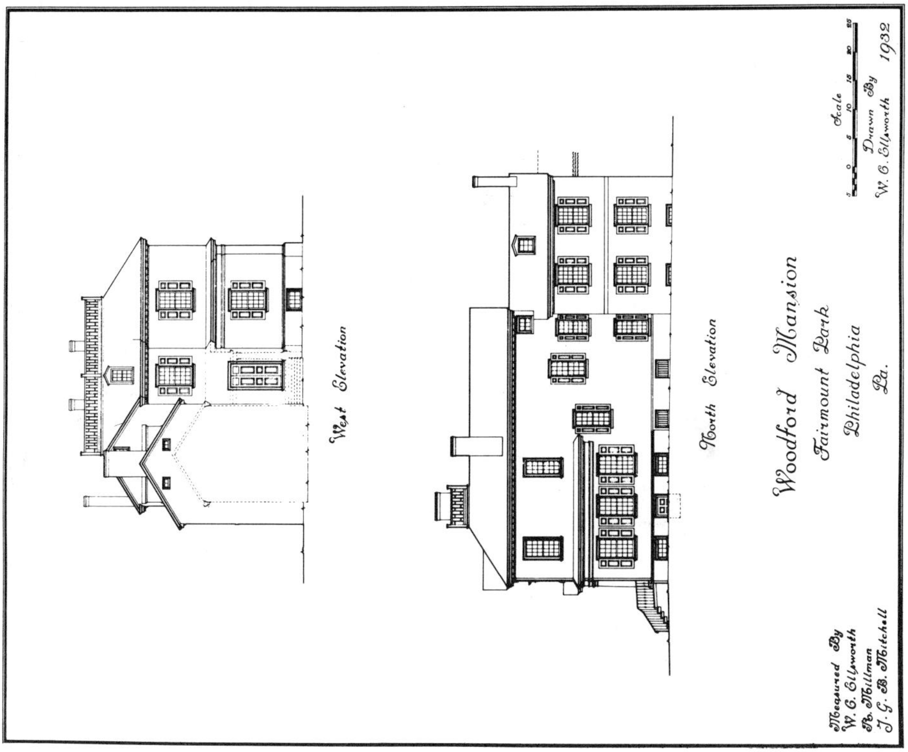

145

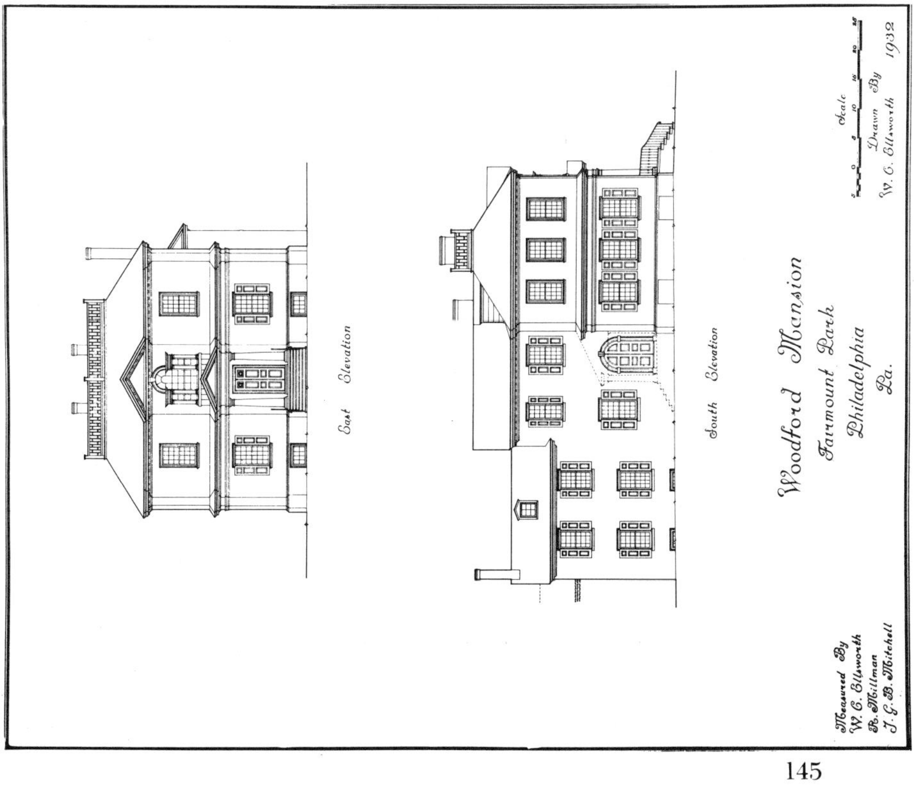

later photographs taken before restoration.[31] All the changes would have accommodated a resident farmer-superintendent.

At about 1870 the property was entered by a driveway leading straight from the Ridge (formerly Wissahickon) Road past the north side of the mansion and behind it to the stable, with offshoots for the numerous outbuildings and for a walk from the stable area to the front entrance which was carried around close to the garden side of the house. A separate, presumably dirt roadway also led back in roughly the line of present-day Dauphin Street to Edgeley nearer the river, with an offshoot as a rear entrance into the Woodford working area.[32]

The whole assemblage never squarely faced the line of the Wissahickon Road. This is confirmed on the early detailed map. Reasons associated with the ground may have dictated to the architect that the mansion should be placed as it now lies. Rock may have been encountered. Topographic maps show that the land began to fall immediately at the rear of the original house and dropped more sharply from just beyond the back edge of the improvements to a ravine and stream both present today.[33] Thus the mansion was placed as far as possible toward the river on the flat land extending back from the public road. Actually the house sits about midway between present-day Ridge Avenue, its former point of entry, and the Schuylkill. A new minor roadway inside the Park has been inserted between Woodford and Ridge Avenue bringing the house much closer to the public viewer than it was built to be and necessitating a greatly shortened front approach and driveway.

With acquisition of the entire property by the City of Philadelphia, Woodford's boundaries extended at their southeast corner out beyond Thirty-third Street, the boundary of the Park at that point; but it is unfortunate that its boundaries inside the Park were obliterated and its separate identity lost. Peculiarly, the authorities paid great attention to woodlands and mapped even individual trees then existing on the site of the acquired properties; but they consciously abandoned their fences and roadways in favor of newly-prepared road schemes leading the public through a unified Park area.

The installation of the Fairmount Park trolley raised the ground level considerably around the old servants' house, which today lies partially in a hollow. Probably during the Fairmount

Park period a tin roof was installed over the original shingles of the mansion. Many other changes must have been made to accommodate the uses to which Woodford was put as the home of the Park Superintendent, headquarters of the Park Guard, the home of the bicycle-mounted and horse-mounted constabulary, a courtroom, and a temporary jail. Various stable extensions, privies and the like cluttered the area.

But shabbiness did not equate with destruction. The fabric was well preserved, perhaps because of its continuous use, at the same time that, in small detail, it was found by Mr. Huntoon to be in a "poor state." New floors were installed. New glass was brought into the windows, although some very early panes have survived intact which include scratchings of names and dates. Interior doors and moldings were replaced, several new window sashes were installed, and a small existing first floor room off the stairhall was converted into a storage closet. A separate bathroom, installed on the second floor between the stairwell and the "ballroom," probably replaced earlier bathing arrangements at the same spot. A proposed division of the "ballroom" into two smaller rooms for custodial use, shown upon the architect's plans, was not carried out.

The 1928 changes slightly altered the outer aspect of Woodford. The old rear porch, all of which had disappeared prior to the restoration, was replaced with the existing small one serving as a linkage of the front and stair halls. A brick walk was installed leading back from the new porch to what was becoming a parking area for automobiles, blocked from any front entry. A new two-story brick extension was added at the rear of the mansion house in place of the earlier shed, providing a modern kitchen, bedroom and bath for custodians. Even though placed on the lower level of the original "backbuildings," this ended four steps above ground at the rear. The old flue and chimney at the rear of the mansion were rebuilt to accommodate the new central furnace. The roof was replaced with asbestos tile shingling.

The original paint colors used in the various rooms were located beneath numerous additional coats.[34] The only items found from earlier days were the fire tongs, fire shovel, and brass jamb hooks still in use at the parlor fireplace.

Except for removal of the stable sheds, the restoration did not extend to it or to the servants' house. In any case the stable had only recently been repaired, because the only known fire in Woodford's history had burned out its upper story and roof in 1925.[35] Hay stored in the loft without adequate ventilation probably created fire by spontaneous combustion. Traces of this can still be seen. It appears that in the rebuilding, vents were opened in the gables and a ventilated cupola was substituted for an earlier one.

The year 1962[36] saw major changes in the arrangements for traffic at the mansion. The front driveway was brought back in a new version extending only the short distance from the inner public road fronting the mansion, and the old rear driveway and

Servants' house after 1975-76 restoration

parking area were paved. The concrete sidewalk approaching the front facade from the south was removed when the new walkway was laid to the front steps in the following year. The visitor could once again enter Woodford as its builders and owners did; and motor traffic could enter at the front or back. The stairwell porch which had served as the entrance since the restoration of 1928 was now little used.

The City's preparations for the Bicentennial in 1975 included the most recent structural changes made at Woodford. The mansion received a new balustrade for its "captain's walk" in the Chippendale form of the original, copied from the watercolor and the painting of Woodford. The original form had been replaced with a simplified one of vertical lines. The servants' house was restored to its original outline by removal of both the front porch and the back shed, a new wood shingle roof was installed, the fireplaces (most of which had been removed at some time) restored, and the chimney extended. A modern kitchen and bathroom were installed; the door to the former shed was blocked up. The stable, a rare surviving form, was left untouched. Importantly, a new boundary line was developed for the Woodford complex and a fence of steel pickets and (at the rear) wire mesh was installed. This restored the feeling of an individual property, rather than simply three buildings standing in the wide expanse of the Park; albeit a far smaller area than that within the old property lines. Also, in preparation for the heavy Bicentennial visitation the trustees installed air conditioning.

So stands Woodford today, awaiting restoration of its rare stable.

Notes

Chapter 1

1. Biographical material respecting Naomi Wood has been taken from Ida May Watson to John P. B. Sinkler, Jan. 23 and Feb. 10, 1945, Naomi Wood Trust records; John P. B. Sinkler, *The Naomi Wood Collection Woodford Mansion* (Phila., 1947). See also "Court Approves Trusteeship for Old Woodford Mansion," *Philadelphia Bulletin*, Aug. 22, 1948.
2. Deed Paoli Knights Land Co. to Susan A. Wood, June 30, 1908, Chester County Recorder of Deeds, Book L13, 486.
3. M. Rodman Street, "A Dutch Colonial House at Paoli," *Philadelphia Suburban Life* (Oct. 1909): 1.
4. Huntoon biographical material has been taken from Talbot Aldrich, biography, sent to John P. B. Sinkler Nov. 5, 1945, Naomi Wood Trust records.
5. Deed Susan A. Wood to Theodore H. Weisenburg, Sep. 9, 1912, Chester County Recorder of Deeds, Book Y13, 246.
6. *Philadelphia Record*, 1912, advertisement by Wm. H. Wilson and Co., Phila., for sale of property Darby Road, Paoli.
7. Codicil to Jan. 13, 1910 Will of Naomi Wood, Estate of Naomi Wood records, Supreme Court of District of Columbia, No. 34,937 (at Clerk of Probate Court, D.C.).
8. Naomi Wood notebook of antique styles and objects, and original invoices for purchases of antiques, Naomi Wood Trust records.
9. Ida May Watson, note 1 above.
10. Petition of executors for instructions, filed June 23, 1927, Estate of Naomi Wood, note 7 above.
11. Naomi Wood to Girard Trust Company, Feb. 22, 1920, and to Huntoon & Co., Mar. 3, 1923, and Daniel T. V. Huntoon memorandum, Sep. 1914, Naomi Wood Trust records.
12. Bernard Quaritch, London, invoices to Naomi Wood, in Paris, France, Nov. 4, 1924.
13. Naomi Wood Trust records.
14. The original Will is in Estate No. 34,937, note 7 above.
15. Petition of executors, note 10 above.
16. "Historic Mansions in Fairmount Park Being Rehabilitated," *Philadelphia Inquirer*, Jan. 17, 1926.
17. Fiske Kimball to Charles E. Peterson, Nov. 19, 1954, Philadelphia Museum of Art, file "Woodford." George and Mary Roberts, *Triumph on Fairmount* (Phila., 1959), 49–51 contains a somewhat different account.
18. The Kimball letter, note 17 above, recounts the progress of restoration of the mansions in some detail, beginning "before 1925."
19. Minutes, Fairmount Park Commission, Mar. 9, 1927, 44.
20. "People Who Live in the Park," *Philadelphia Record*, Aug. 11, 1898.
21. "Old Fairmount Park Mansion Begin Restored," *Philadelphia Inquirer*, Dec. 2, 1928; and see "Court Approves Trusteeship for Old Woodford Mansion," *Philadelphia Bulletin*, Aug. 22, 1948.
22. Aldrich, note 4 above; Huntoon to Commissioners, Mar. 1, 1927 and Dec. 7, 1934, Naomi Wood Trust records.
23. Huntoon Woodford scrapbook, Naomi Wood Trust records.
24. Minutes, Fairmount Park Commission, July 13, 1927, 456.
25. Petition of executors, note 10 above.
26. Order of Supreme Court of District of Columbia, June 24, 1927, Estate No. 34,937, note 7 above.

Chapter 2

1. Sam Bass Warner, Jr., *The Private City* (Phila., 1968), 16.
2. Brief of Title to Woodford, Feb. 16, 1869, Philadelphia City Archives, file "Woodford" (hereafter cited as "Pha. Arch. Wdfd."); W. H. Hornor, Jr., "Woodford" in "Men and Things," *Philadelphia Bulletin*, Jan. 9, 1930.
3. *Pennsylvania Gazette* (Philadelphia), Mar. 6, 1756. Survey by John Lukens, July, 1760, Pha. Arch. Wdfd., shows the tract.

NOTES 151

4. See recitals in deed Samuel Morris, Sheriff, to William Coleman, July 19, 1756, Philadelphia Recorder of Deeds, Book I6, 522.
5. Samuel Wetherill, Jr., insurance survey "Alexander Barclay's Country Seat," 9th mo. 5th, 1769, Philadelphia Contributionship.
6. John F. Watson, *Annals of Philadelphia and Pennsylvania, In the Olden Time* (Phila., 1877 ed.) 1: 53, 444, 600.
7. Will of Thomas Bradford, Philadelphia Register of Wills, Book D, 271.
8. Charles E. Peterson, *The Carpenters' Company 1786 Rule Book* (Princeton, 1971), iii.
9. Incidents in Coleman's life are sometimes taken from Whitfield J. Bell, Jr., unpublished biography prepared for American Philosophical Society, 1969, and authorities there cited.
10. *Benjamin Franklin's Autobiographical Writings*, ed. Carl Van Doren (New York, 1945), 260.
11. *Ibid.*, 622.
12. *Pa. Gazette*, Jan. 19, 1769.
13. *Franklin's Autobiographical Writings*, 259–260.
14. *Philadelphia Monthly Meeting Minutes* (Marriages 1672–1871), at Historical Society of Pennsylvania (hereafter cited as "HSP"), 102.
15. George E. McCracken, *The Welcome Claimants Proved, Disproved and Doubtful* (Baltimore, 1970), 2: 191.
16. See *Ibid.*, 197–198. Biographical data respecting the Fitzwaters has also been taken from unpublished materials prepared by Mildred F. Fisher.
17. Thompson Westcott, *A History of Philadelphia* (Phila. Sunday Dispatch, 1867) (hereafter "Westcott, *History*"), ch. 128.
18. McCracken, *The Welcome Claimants*, 202–203, 208.
19. *Franklin's Autobiographical Writings*, 43.
20. See *The Papers of Benjamin Franklin*, eds. Leonard W. Labaree and Whitfield J. Bell, Jr. (New Haven, 1961), 3: 221–223 and Westcott, *History*, chs. 101–103, respecting *The Warren* and the Association Battery lottery.
21. *Franklin's Autobiographical Writings*, 66–67.
22. Nicholas B. Wainwright, *A Philadelphia Story. The Philadelphia Contributionship* (Phila., 1952), 28, 30, 34.
23. *Franklin's Autobiographical Writings*, 49, 260.
24. *Pa. Gazette*, Apr. 13, 1758.
25. Nov. 18, 1748, HSP Manuscript Collections (hereafter "HSP MS Collns."), Pemberton Papers.
26. Richard Peters to Thomas Penn, 2 8ber, 1756, *Pennsylvania Magazine of History and Biography* (hereafter "*PMHB*") 31 (1907): 246.
27. Westcott, *History*, ch. 152.
28. *Idem*.
29. *Gentleman's Magazine* (London, Dec., 1769), 567, 638.
30. Watson, *Annals of Philadelphia*, 1: 144; Gunning Bedford, insurance survey of property of Coleman, Second and Pine Streets, Dec. 1766, Philadelphia Contributionship.
31. Nicholas B. Wainwright, *Colonial Grandeur in Philadelphia* (Phila., 1964), 8, 152.
32. *Pa. Gazette*, Mar. 31, 1768.
33. *Ibid.*, Oct. 20, 1768.
34. Philadelphia Register of Wills, Book O, 315.
35. Inventory, Register of Wills, Feb. 10, 1769, Estate No. 235 of 1769.
36. *Pa. Gazette*, Jan. 19, 1769.

Chapter 3

1. *Pa. Gazette*, May 11, 1769, Supp.
2. Biographical facts respecting Alexander Barclay are sometimes taken from Gertrude Thomas' unpublished article on his life. And see Gregory B. Keen, "The Descendants of Joran Kyn, The Founder of Upland," *PMHB* 5 (1881): 85, 96 and note.
3. "Collectors of Customs at Philadelphia," *PMHB* 25 (1901): 576; Westcott, *History*, ch. 209, p. 445.

4. For Barclay's biography see *Encyclopaedia Brittanica* (11th ed., 1910), "Robert Barclay"; *Dictionary of National Biography* (hereafter "DNB") (London, 1885), 3: "Robert Barclay"; Townsend Ward, "Second Street and the Second Street Road," *PMHB* 4 (1880): 401, 429.
5. Keen, "Descendants of Joran Kyn," 96.
6. Beverly McAnear, "An American In London . . .," *PMHB* 64 (1940): 186 note 27.
7. To James Pemberton, Nov. 12, 1761, HSP MS Collns.
8. *Pa. Gazette*, Sep. 16, 1756.
9. Wainwright, *Colonial Grandeur in Philadelphia*, 5.
10. *Pennsylvania Archives*, 2nd Series, VIII: 14.
11. *PMHB* 6 (1882): 256.
12. *Pa. Gazette*, Jan. 22, 1761.
13. Thomas Willing Balch, "The Swift Family of Philadelphia," *PMHB* 30 (1906): 135, 136.
14. Frank M. Etting, *An Historical Account of The Old State House of Pennsylvania* (Phila., 1891), 47–55.
15. *Ibid.*, 53; Westcott, *History*, ch. 155.
16. To John Swift, Alexander Barclay and Thomas Graeme, HSP MS Collns.
17. Westcott, *History*, ch. 157, p. 354; Etting, *The Old State House*, 58.
18. *Ibid.*, 62–63.
19. See also Westcott, *History*, ch. 160, p. 360.
20. *Ibid.*, ch. 161, p. 362.
21. Deed, executors of William Coleman to Alexander Barclay, Deed Book I6, 483, and Mortgage, Alexander and Rebecca Barclay to the executors, both May 18, 1769; Brief of Title; all at Pha. Arch. Wdfd.
22. Samuel Wetherill, Jr., insurance survey of Woodford, 9th mo. 5th, 1769, Philadelphia Contributionship; Minutes of the Directors, Sep. 5, 1769.
23. Westcott, *History*, ch. 161, p. 362.
24. Etting, 192–193.
25. Balch, "The Swift Family," 143.
26. Letters by David Barclay, David and John Barclay, Alexander's son Robert Barclay, and Rebecca Barclay, identified in the text or the notes by date, are indexed at HSP MS Collns.
27. Estate of Alexander Barclay, Account of executors, 1771, Philadelphia Register of Wills, Administration No. 12 of 1771.
28. *Pa. Gazette*, Jan. 17, 1771.
29. *Ibid.*, June 13, 1771; deed Judah Foulke to David Franks, July 18, 1771, Philadelphia Recorder of Deeds, Book B3, 144, at Pha. Arch. Wdfd.
30. Account of executors, note 27 above.
31. John W. Jordan, *Colonial Families of Philadelphia* (New York, 1911), 1: 8.
32. Will of Alexander Barclay, Philadelphia County Will Book P, 38 (microfilm no. 246 of 1771); Inventory, Jan. 20, 1771, No. 26 of 1771.
33. Robert, Aug. 22, 1771; Jan. 7, 1773; July 21, 1773; May 23, 1774 (to Thomas Parke); Feb. 22, 1775; David Barclay to James Pemberton, Feb. 10, 1773.
34. Robert, Jan. 7, 1773; David Barclay, Feb. 18, 1773 and Feb. 1, 1775.
35. David Barclay to James Pemberton, Feb. 5, 1775; Robert, Sep. 3, 1775.
36. David and John Barclay, Jan. 7, 1772; Robert, Aug. 22, 1771 and Dec. 4, 1771.
37. Jan. 7, 1773; Sep. 3, 1775; Dec. 22, 1775; Jan. 10, 1778.
38. Keen, "Descendants of Joran Kyn," 96–97.
39. Robert, Dec. 21, 1775; Mar. 16, 1776.
40. Robert, May 31, 1783.
41. James Boswell, *The Life of Samuel Johnson* (London, 1853 ed.), 8: 61 and note.
42. Data respecting the later life of Robert Barclay is taken from the unpublished file of The American Philosophical Society, "Robert Barclay."

Chapter 4

1. Edwin Wolf 2nd, "Abigail Evans Franks' Bible," *American Jewish Historical Quarterly* 8 (1968): 137.
2. *The Lee Max Friedman Collection of American Jewish Colonial Correspondence*, eds. Leo Hershkowitz and Isidore S. Meyer (American Jewish Historical Society Publica-

tion No. 5, Waltham, Mass., 1968), xvi (hereafter "Hershkowitz").
3. *Ibid.*, 5.
4. *Ibid.*, 15.
5. *Ibid.*, 71; and see 49, note 21.
6. Edwin Wolf 2nd and Maxwell Whiteman, *The history of the Jews of Philadelphia from Colonial times to the Age of Jackson* (Phila., 1956), 26, 27, 38, 387 note 17 (hereafter "Wolf"). The family's unusual mobility may have had to do with its obtaining portraits of its children. See Hannah R. London, *Portraits of Jews by Gilbert Stuart and other Early American Artists* (New York, 1927), 8–15, 74; *Early American Jewish Portraiture* (catalogue, American Jewish Historical Society, New York, 1952), 11.
7. Hershkowitz, 102 and note 113; Wolf, 27.
8. Victor Rosewater, *The Liberty Bell Its History and Significance* (New York, 1926), 8; Wolf, 27, 29 and 388 notes 20, 21.
9. For date of David Franks' marriage, see Hershkowitz, 129 note 3. And see Dennis, note 10 below, 638.
10. Jessie McNab Dennis, "Franks family silver by Lamerie," *Antiques Magazine* (May, 1968): 636; and see Hershkowitz, 131 notes.
11. *Ibid.*, 114, 129 note 3.
12. *Ibid.*, 116–117, and note 4.
13. Henry Russell Drowne, "Fraunces Tavern," *Sons of the Revolution Quarterly* (1933).
14. Wolf, 29, 38.
15. Etting, *The Old State House*, 34–35; Westcott, *History*, ch. 135, p. 321; Wolf, 30.
16. Wolf, 38, 391 note 9.
17. Harold E. Gillingham, "Indian Silver Ornaments," *PMHB* 58 (1934): 97, 109–110; Peters, Mar. 1, 1759, HSP MS Collns.
18. Etting, *The Old State House*, bet. 51–52.
19. Will of David Franks, note 70 below; Wolf, 66–74.
20. Thompson Westcott, *The Historical Mansions and Buildings of Philadelphia* (Phila., 1877), 416–417, 419, 421–422.
21. Deed Judah Foulke to David Franks, July 18, 1771, Philadelphia Recorder of Deeds, Book B3, 144, and Mortgage David and Margaret Franks; both at Pha. Arch. Wdfd.
22. Gunning Bedford, insurance survey of Woodford, Nov. 3, 1772, Philadelphia Contributionship.
23. Warner, *The Private City* (Phila., 1968), 9.
24. City and County of Philadelphia tax lists, 1769 and 1774, Pha. Arch.
25. Robert F. Oaks, "Big Wheels in Philadelphia," *PMHB* 90 (1971): 351; "An Account of Coaches . . . in Philadelphia," *PMHB* 27 (1903): 375.
26. Warner, *The Private City*, 9.
27. Joseph Jackson, *Encyclopedia of Philadelphia* (Harrisburg, 1931), 3: "James Logan"; Frederick B. Tolles, "Town House and Country House . . .," *PMHB* 82 (1958): 397, 398, 400.
28. Nicholas B. Wainwright, "A Diary of Trifling Occurrences," *PMHB* 82 (1958): 411, 418 and note.
29. Wolf, 86, 404 note 49.
30. *Ibid.*, 86.
31. Daniel Chamiers to David Franks, Feb. 1776 and Feb. 25, 1777; Washington to President of Congress, Feb. 14, 1776; HSP MS. Collns.
32. Wolf, 87.
33. Westcott, *History*, ch. 251, p. 520.
34. Feb. 26, 1778, *PMHB* 16 (1892): 216–218.
35. John McAllister, Jr., unpublished MS, 1860, collection of the authors. And see Frederick D. Stone, "Philadelphia Society One Hundred Years Ago . . .," *PMHB* 3 (1879): 361, 367.
36. Westcott, *History*, ch. 260, p. 536.
37. Gratz Mordecai, *Notice of Jacob Mordecai* (American Jewish Historical Society Publication No. 6, 1897), 32, 40, 41; and see London, *Portraits of Jews*, 74; James T. Flexner, *The Traitor and the Spy* (New York, 1953), 41, 139; Stephen Birmingham, *The Grandees* (New York, 1971), 166.
38. Robert Barclay to Thomas Parke, Mar. 30, 1777, HSP MS Collns.

39. André's own description of the Mischianza (so spelled by him) appears in Westcott, *History*, ch. 261. For a secondary account see Elizabeth F. Ellet, *The Women of the American Revolution* (New York, 1848), 1: 182–187.
40. Westcott, *History*, ch. 261, p. 539.
41. Ellet, 1: 179; Stone, "Philadelphia Society," 364.
42. Watson, *Annals of Philadelphia*, 2: 297.
43. Ellet, 1: 188; Flexner, 226; Stone, 364.
44. Rebecca Franks to Elizabeth Shippen, "Thursday Noon," reprinted in Lewis Burd Walker, "Life of Margaret Shippen, Wife of Benedict Arnold," *PMHB* 24 (1900): 401, 417.
45. Westcott, *History*, ch. 265, p. 547.
46. Oct. 18, 1778, HSP MS Collns.
47. *Journals of the Continental Congress 1774–1789*, 12:1032–1033.
48. *Ibid.*, 1038, 1070, 1076, 1110.
49. *Minutes of Supreme Executive Council of Pennsylvania* (Harrisburg, 1852), 11: 679, 682–683.
50. See Wolf, 90.
51. *Minutes of Supreme Executive Council* (Harrisburg, 1853), 12: 195, 199, 206.
52. *Ibid.*, 495, 499, 501, 505. Petition is in HSP MS Collns.
53. *Ibid.*, 509.
54. *Pennsylvania Packet* (Philadelphia), Oct. 31, 1780; Wolf, 92. These and other volumes signed by Franks are in the library at Cliveden, Philadelphia, property of the National Trust for Historic Preservation.
55. Lorenzo Sabine, *Biographical Sketches of Loyalists of the American Revolution* (Boston, 1864, reprint Port Washington, N.Y., 1966), 1: 445; *Minutes of Executive Council*, 12: 547.
56. Deed Philadelphia Recorder of Deeds, Book 2, 462; Mortgage David and Margaret Franks to Thomas Paschall, Dec. 21, 1775; both at Pha. Arch. Wdfd.
57. Franks to Bernard Gratz, Nov. 22, 1780, HSP MS Collns.
58. Morris Jastrow, *Notes on the Jews of Philadelphia, from Published Annals* (American Jewish Historical Society Publication No. 1, 1892), 55.
59. To Messrs. Coxe and Hamilton, May 10, 1782, HSP MS Collns.
60. To Messrs. Coxe and Hamilton, Sep. 2, 1782, HSP MS Collns.
61. Jastrow, 55–56.
62. To Joseph Simons, July 28, 1783, HSP MS Collns.
63. Wolf, 181; Power of Attorney, Mar. 20, 1786, Philadelphia Recorder of Deeds, Book D17, 503.
64. Horace E. Hayden, "The Reminiscences of David Hayfield Conyingham," *Wyoming Historical and Genealogical Society Proceedings* 8 (1904): 181, 249.
65. From Philadelphia, to Joseph Simons, Sep. 4, 1789, HSP MS Collns.
66. Wolf, 136.
67. *Ibid.*, 389 note 48; Henry S. Morais, *The Jews of Philadelphia* (Phila., 1894), 35 (an affidavit by Franks).
68. *Letters of Benjamin Rush*, ed. Lyman H. Butterfield (Princeton, 1951), 2: 714–715; Matthew Carey, *A Short Account of the Yellow Fever* (Phila., 1794), 16: Wolf, 195, 438 note 57.
69. The estate of another David Franks was opened in Philadelphia in May, 1792 (No. 101); but David Franks of Woodford's affidavit in the federal court at Philadelphia was taken on December 26th of that year. See also Hershkowitz, 3 note 8, and 113 note 6.
70. Lothrop Withington, "Pennsylvania Gleanings in England," *PMHB* 29 (1905): 310, 315.

Chapter 5

1. To Betsy Shippen, "Friday night," HSP MS Collns., Shippen papers.
2. Westcott, *History*, ch. 172, note p. 383, and ch. 256, p. 528.
3. Rebecca Franks to Anne Harrison Paca, Feb. 26, 1778, *PMHB* 16 (1892): 216–218.
4. Joseph J. Kelley, Jr., *Life and Times in Colonial Philadelphia* (Harrisburg, Pa., 1973), 167.
5. *Ibid.*, 177.

6. John W. Jordan, *Colonial Families of Philadelphia*, 1: 8–9.
7. Letter note 3 above includes the last four quotations.
8. Gregory A. Stiverson and Phebe R. Jacobsen, *William Paca, A Biography* (Baltimore, 1976), 81.
9. Westcott, *History*, ch. 256, p. 529 and note.
10. *Ibid.*, p. 528.
11. Birmingham, *The Grandees*, 173.
12. Kelley, *Life and Times*, 178.
13. "Thursday Noon," reprinted in Walker, "Life of Margaret Shippen," *PMHB* 24 (1900): 401, 417.
14. Kelley, 178.
15. See Flexner, *The Traitor and the Spy*, 210.
16. Westcott, *History*, ch. 261, note p. 540, and ch. 218, note.
17. Letter, note 3 above; Westcott, *History*, ch. 424, p. 841.
18. Letter, note 13 above.
19. Ellet, *Women of the Revolution*, 1: 179; Max J. Kohler, *Rebecca Franks An American Jewish Belle of the Last Century* (New York, 1894), 20.
20. Kelley, 184.
21. Ellet, 1: 180; Kohler, 20.
22. Kelley, 210–211.
23. *Idem;* John R. Alden, *General Charles Lee* (Baton Rouge, La., 1951), 270–273; Westcott, *History*, ch. 393, pp. 753–754.
24. Kohler, 20.
25. Peter Kemble could well have known Rebecca, but his grandson appears mistaken in saying *he* had seen her, for she left for England in 1782 and is not known to have returned; while Gouverneur Kemble was born in 1786. His tale has the ring of truth, however. Rebecca could have returned in connection with her father's death in 1793 or that of her sister Abigail in September, 1798.
26. For the poem and surrounding circumstances, see "A Loyalist's Poem," ed. Benson J. Lossing, *American Historical Record* 2 (1873): 390–392, 438–441, 491–493; also Kohler, 14–18, 26 note.
27. Letter to Abigail Hamilton, Aug. 10, 1781, *PMHB* 23 (1899): 303–309.
28. Ellet, 1: 178–179.
29. See Hershkowitz, 116 note.
30. This and the three following quotations are taken from letter, note 27 above, and are illustrative of Rebecca's character, perceptiveness, and use of language.
31. Westcott, *History*, ch. 424, p. 841.
32. Townsend Ward, "A Walk to Darby," *PMHB* 3 (1879): 150, 162.
33. Kohler, 32.
34. Henry B. Dawson, *The Assault on Stony Pont, by General Anthony Wayne* (Morrisania, N.Y., 1863), 103.
35. *DNB*, 5: "Sir Henry Johnson."
36. Benson J. Lossing, *Field Book of the American Revolution* (New York, 1855), 1: 744; Stone, "Philadelphia Society," 363 note. For a contemporary account see "Letters from William Franklin to William Strahan," ed. Charles Henry Hart, *PMHB* 35 (1911): 415, 455.
37. Johnson to Washington, July 20, 1779, HSP MS Collns.; Dawson, 84.
38. Edwin Wolf 2nd, *Annual Report of the Library Company of Philadelphia for 1974* (Phila., 1975), 50–51.
39. *DNB*, note 35 above.
40. Ellet, 1: 178, 181.
41. Winfield Scott, *Memoirs* (New York, 1864), 1: 171–174.
42. *Burke's Peerage* (London, 1967), "Johnson of Bath."
43. There is some difference of opinion as to Rebecca's age, but calculation has been made on the basis of Wolf, "Abigail Evans Franks' Bible," above. See Stanley F. Chyet, "Rebecca Franks," in *Notable American Women*, ed. Edward T. James (Cambridge, Mass., 1971), 665–666, and notes there appended; also *Gentleman's Magazine* (March, 1823), obituary.
44. John East, Curate, St. Michael with St. Paul, Bath, letter November, 1977, in Naomi Wood Trust records.

Chapter 6

1. Executors of William Coleman, Release of Mortgage to Thomas Paschall, Apr. 20, 1782, endorsed on deed David Franks to Paschall Nov. 22, 1780, Pha. Arch. Wdfd.
2. John J. Parker, *Descendants of Thomas Paschall and Joanna Sloper* (at Chester County, Pa., Historical Society, undated) 17, 19.
3. *Philadelphia Monthly Meeting Records,* 134, 338, 339, 351, 466, HSP.
4. Jackson, *Encyclopedia of Philadelphia,* 4: "Paschallville." And see William B. Campbell, *Old Towns and Districts of Philadelphia* (City History Society, Phila., 1942), 118.
5. McCracken, *The Welcome Claimants,* 313–317; Ledlie I. Laughlin, *Pewter in America* (Boston, 1940), 2: 37.
6. *Abstract of a Letter from Thomas Paschall of Pennsylvania . . . ,* broadside, London, 1683, HSP MS Collns., Broadside Index; and see *PMHB* 6 (1882): 323.
7. Howard W. Lloyd, *Lloyd Family Manuscripts* (Lancaster, Pa., 1912), 226–232; Robert C. Moon, *The Morris Family of Philadelphia* (Phila., 1898), 2: 545, 549; John W. Jordan, *Colonial Families of Philadelphia,* 1: 653; Wilfred Jordan, *Colonial and Revolutionary Families of Pennsylvania* (New York, 1934), 5: 656, 657.
8. Thomas Paschall, Malt and Barley Record Book, *Guide to the Manuscript Collections of HSP* (hereafter "*HSP MS Guide*") (Phila., 1949), item no. 1530.
9. See Jackson, *Encyclopedia,* 1: "Blockley."
10. Watson, *Annals of Philadelphia,* 3: 423; Thomas A. Glenn, *Some Colonial Mansions and Those Who Lived in Them* (Phila., 1899), 1: 112; John W. Jordan, *Colonial Families,* 1: 653.
11. Parker, *Descendants of Thomas Paschall,* 49.
12. *Philadelphia Monthly Meeting Records,* 134.
13. *Philadelphia City Directories,* 1785 (White), 1791, 1795, 1796; *U.S. Census* (1790), 220.
14. Westcott, *History,* ch. 155, p. 350.
15. Thomas Paschall, Ledger 1767–1770, HSP MS Collns., Case 64.
16. Westcott, *History,* ch. 251, p. 520.
17. Thompson Westcott, *Names of Persons Who Took the Oath of Allegiance* (Phila., 1865), 44.
18. Inventory, Estate of Thomas Paschall, Apr. 5, 1796, *HSP MS Guide,* item no. 1587.
19. *Philadelphia Monthly Meeting Records,* 134.
20. *Ibid.,* 499. Will and Codicil of Paschall, Philadelphia Register of Wills, Book X, 423, Estate no. 273 of 1796. His silhouette illustrated herein is in HSP, Society Silhouette Collection, Perot Division.
21. Hayden, "Reminiscences of David Hayfield Conyngham," 195–199, 238; John W. Jordan, *Colonial Families,* 1: 774–776.
22. Westcott, *Historic Mansions of Philadelphia,* 280–283; Westcott, *History,* ch. 270; Kelley, *Life and Times,* 218.
23. Hayden, "Reminiscences of Conyngham," 221 and note.
24. Watson, *Annals,* 3: 555. Conyngham maintained a city home in Front Street, *U.S. Census* (1790), 236.
25. Townsend Ward, "The Germantown Road and Its Associations," *PMHB* 6 (1882): 1, 18 and illustration; Hayden, "Reminiscences of Conyngham," 199.
26. Charles S. Keyser, *Fairmount Park* (Phila., 1871), 70; Frank Cousins and Phil M. Riley, *The Colonial Architecture of Philadelphia* (Boston, 1920), 22; J. Bunford Samuel, *A Word Sketch of Fairmount Park* (Phila., 1926), 13; Harold D. Eberlein and Cortlandt V. Hubbard, *Portrait of a Colonial City* (Phila., 1939), 320; Sarah D. Lowrie, *Strawberry Mansion* (Phila., 1941), 45; Sidney Earle, *History of Fairmount Park* (ca. 1950), typescript at HSP, 95, 98.
27. For biographies see William Primrose, "Biography of William Lewis," *PMHB* 20 (1896): 30; Horace Binney, *Leaders of the Old Bar of Philadelphia* (Phila., 1866), 1–45.
28. Watson, *Annals,* 3: 287.
29. Lowrie, *Strawberry Mansion,* 41.
30. Deed Paschall to Isaac Wharton, Aug. 28, 1793, Philadelphia Recorder of Deeds, Book 42, 379, at Pha. Arch. Wdfd.

Chapter 7

1. Glenn, "Descendants of Francis Rawle," in *Some Colonial Mansions*, 2: 194–195.
2. Inventory of Estate of Isaac Wharton, Philadelphia Register of Wills, Estate no. 42 of 1808, "Country Residence."
3. Deed Johns Hopkins to Isaac Wharton, Apr. 24, 1798, Philadelphia Recorder of Deeds, Book 69, 119, and plan, Reading Howell, Apr. 7, 1798. Survey, John Lukens, July, 1760, shows both the new purchase and the land already owned. All at Pha. Arch. Wdfd.
4. Brief of title to Woodford, Pha. Arch. Wdfd.
5. Anne H. Wharton, *The Wharton Family* (Phila., 1880), 9. For Walnut Grove, see Westcott, *Historic Mansions of Philadelphia*, 466–471.
6. Philadelphia Register of Wills, Book Q, 321.
7. John Hills, Plan of Wharton Properties, Oct. 31, 1789, *HSP MS Guide*, item no. 1091.
8. Watson, *Annals of Philadelphia*, 3: 471; Westcott, *Historic Mansions*, 480.
9. *Sally Wister's Journal*, ed. Albert C. Myers (Phila., 1902), 202, 204. For Laurel Hill, see Glenn, *Some Colonial Mansions*, 2: 123.
10. Marriage Certificate, 11th mo. 14, 1786, HSP MS Collns.
11. Wharton, *The Wharton Family*, 18–19; John W. Jordan, *Colonial Families of Philadelphia*, 1: 540.
12. Wharton, 29.
13. Westcott, *Names of Persons*, 17.
14. *Ibid.*, xvii–xx.
15. Wharton, 12; John W. Jordan, 1: 541.
16. Isaac Wharton, Receipt of Protest, Feb. 9, 1782, and Wharton to Tench Coxe, Feb. 25, 1782, HSP MS Collns.
17. Wharton, 13; John W. Jordan, 1: 542.
18. *Philadelphia City Directories*, 1785, 1795, 1800, 1808; James Logan to Isaac Wharton, Pres., Apr. 17, 1804, HSP MS Collns.
19. Will Book 2, 285, original at Pha. Arch. Wdfd.
20. Westcott, *History*, ch. 422, p. 835; *U.S. Census* (1790), 219.
21. Edward Biddle and Mantle Fielding, *The Life and Work of Thomas Sully* (Phila., 1921), 316–317, illustrated herein.
22. Deed Margaret Rawle Wharton et al. to Francis R. Wharton, Aug. 21, 1809, Philadelphia Recorder of Deeds, Book IC6, 39.
23. Executor's cashbook, Estate no. 42 of 1808; Jackson, *Encyclopedia*, 4: "Ridge Road."
24. J. Thomas Scharf and Thompson Westcott, *History of Philadelphia* (Phila., 1884), 1: 693 note.
25. See Elizabeth B. Clay, "Reliving the Days of Washington," *Ladies' Home Journal* (June, 1932), 14–15.
26. Will Book 47, 230; Brief of Title, Pha. Arch. Wdfd.

Chapter 8

1. Pennsylvania Act of Mar. 26, 1867, P.L. 547.
2. Earle, *History of Fairmount Park*, 11–12; Jackson, *Encyclopedia*, 3: "Fairmount Park," 4: "Water Supply"; Marion W. Rivinus, *The History of the Fairmount Park Guard* (Phila., 1976), 11.
3. Scharf and Westcott, *History of Philadelphia*, 1: 675–676; Pamphlets: *Lemon Hill, in its Connection with the Efforts to Obtain a Public Park* (Phila., 1856); *Sedgeley Park Estate* (Phila., 1857).
4. Thomas Ridgway, Provisional Treasurer, *Fairmount Park Contribution* (Phila., 1856).
5. Charles S. Keyser and Thomas Cochran, *Lemon Hill and Fairmount Park* (Phila., 1856, 1872, reprinted 1886), 4, 8, 10.
6. Jackson, *Encyclopedia*, 4: "Sedgley"; and see George B. Tatum, "The origins of Fairmount Park," *Antiques Magazine* (Nov., 1962), 502.
7. "Plan of Properties Included within the Limits of Fairmount Park," ca. 1867–1868, Fairmount Park Commission.
8. Pennsylvania Act of Apr. 14, 1868, P.L. 1083.

9. See "Map of . . . Fairmount Park . . . 1868," *Second Annual Report of the Commissioners of Fairmount Park* (Phila., 1870), frontispiece.
10. Mar. 6, 1869, Deed Book JTO-207, 123, 130; both deeds at Pha. Arch. Wdfd.
11. Rivinus, *Fairmount Park Guard*, 13.
12. *Annual Report of the Commissioners of Fairmount Park* (Phila., 1878), 49, 51, 53, 64.
13. (Phila., 1871), 51.
14. For biographical facts respecting Cresson, see Frederick Fraley, "Obituary Notice of John C. Cresson," *American Philosophical Society Proceedings* (Phila., Oct. 19, 1877), 149–162.
15. (Phila., 1870), 37. No such separate map has been located.
16. Russell Thayer family records, Mrs. William H. Reeves, unpublished.
17. *Sixth Report of the Commissioners* (Phila., 1899), 21–22.
18. *Annual Report* (1878), 60–64.
19. See *Reports of Commissioners: Third*, 34–35; *of 1878*, 52; *Fourth*, 35–36; *Sixth*, 8, 22.
20. Rivinus, 5.
21. Harold D. Eberlein and Horace M. Lippincott, *The Colonial Homes of Philadelphia and its Neighbourhood* (Phila., 1912), 140.
22. *Sixth Report*, 10; Act of Apr. 14, 1868, P.L. 1083, section 20; Harold E. Cox, *The Fairmount Park Trolley* (Forty-Fort, Pa., 1970), 7–8.
23. Cox, *Fairmount Park Trolley*, 8.
24. *Ibid.*, 3, 9; *Sixth Report*, 10–11, 40–56.
25. Cox, photos, 18, 27.
26. *Ibid.*, map.
27. *Ibid.*, 11.
28. *Ibid.*, 29, 31.
29. *Sixth Report*, 21–22.
30. "Old Fairmount Park Mansion Being Restored," *Philadelphia Inquirer*, Dec. 2, 1928.
31. *Report of Commissioners for 1912*, 7.
32. *Sixth Report*, 94.
33. *Reports of Commissioners: 1912*, 7; *1913*, 13; *1878*, 37; *1916*, 7.
34. Memorandum in Fiske Kimball, personal file "Woodford," Philadelphia Museum of Art.
35. Plan by John D. Estabrook, at Fairmount Park Commission.
36. "Destroying Park Monarch," *Philadelphia Record*, May 27, 1912.
37. *Report of Chief Engineer for 1912*, 24. Herbert C. Wise and H. F. Beidleman, *Colonial Architecture for Those About to Build* (Phila., 1913), 45, reported that the parlor ceiling was renewed in 1911 and that the parlor in these years was "grained a yellow colour."
38. "Woodford Gets Her Face Lifted," *Philadelphia Record*, May 22, 1943.

Chapter 9

1. Biography of John P. B. Sinkler, American Institute of Architects, Philadelphia Chapter, unpublished typescript.
2. *Philadelphia Inquirer*, Dec. 2, 1928.
3. Joseph Downs to John P. B. Sinkler, Nov. 15, 1928; Calvin Hathaway to Fiske Kimball, Sep. 13, 1930; Philadelphia Museum of Art, file "Woodford."
4. Mar. 31, 1930.
5. Daniel T. V. Huntoon notebook, memoranda and inventories, Naomi Wood Trust records.
6. Sarah D. Lowrie, "As One Woman Sees It," *Pulbic Ledger*, May 22, 1932.
7. *The Pennsylvania Museum Bulletin* (Oct.–Nov., 1928), 27, 29; (Dec., 1928), 31.
8. Memorandum, Feb. 1937, and letter to Fairmount Park Commissioners, Dec. 7, 1934, Naomi Wood Trust records.
9. "Rare Collection Gets Home in Park," note 4 above.
10. "Ancient Mansion Open," *Philadelphia Bulletin*, Apr. 12, 1930; "Woodford," Apr. 16, 1930; "Woodford House, Restored Colonial Mansion is Opened," *Philadelphia Record*, Apr. 12, 1930.
11. *Reports of the Chief Engineer to Fairmount Park Commission: for 1928*, 4; *for 1930*, 4; *for 1932*, 4.

12. Francis B. Brandt, "Woodford in Fairmount Park," *Public Ledger,* July 23, 1930.
13. "Woodford," May 10, 1931.
14. *Reports of Chief Engineer: for 1931,* 5; *for 1932,* 5.
15. O. Valdes plan, "Woodford Mansion," ca. 1930, showing terminal, at Fairmount Park Commission.
16. Elizabeth B. Clay, "Reliving the Days of Washington," *Ladies' Home Journal* (June, 1932), 14.
17. Huntoon purchase invoices, Naomi Wood Trust records.
18. Especially Talbot Aldrich, unpublished typescript biography (Boston, 1945), Naomi Wood Trust records.
19. Issues of Oct., 1932 and July, 1939.
20. Philadelphia Register of Wills, Book PS 289, 23.
21. For Sinkler's assuming the trusteeship, see "Woodford Gets Her Face Lifted," *Philadelphia Record,* May 22, 1943; "Court Approves Trusteeship for Old Woodford Mansion," *Philadelphia Bulletin,* Aug. 22, 1948.
22. Titled *The Naomi Wood Collection Woodford Mansion.*
23. Will of John P B. Sinkler, June 25, 1958, Philadelphia Register of Wills, Book PS 902, 221.
24. *The Naomi Wood Collection at Woodford Mansion,* undated.
25. "Past and Present Linked in Tours of Colonial Homes," *Philadelphia Inquirer,* June 3, 1960; Ruth Seltzer, "The Philadelphia Scene," *Sunday Bulletin,* June 5, 1960.
26. Ruth Seltzer, "The Philadelphia Scene," *Philadelphia Bulletin,* Apr. 17 and May 4, 1960.
27. See Morrison H. Heckscher, "Furniture of Federal Philadelphia," *The University Hospital Antiques Show 1964* (catalogue, Phila., 1964), 29 and illus., 49.
28. Report, Sep. 29, 1971, Naomi Wood Trust Records.
29. Martin P. Snyder, "Woodford," 515.
30. June Avery Snyder and Martin P. Snyder, "Woodford Celebrates the Bicentennial," *Pennsylvania Heritage* (Harrisburg, June, 1977), 20. June Avery Snyder, "Rebecca Franks: Witty, Clever Tory Belle," in *The Founding City,* eds. David R. Boldt and Willard F. Randall (Radnor, Pa., 1976), 67, and in "Bicentennial Journal," *Philadelphia Inquirer,* Mar. 15, 1976; "Museum Know-How," *Antique Collector* (London, Feb. 1980), 50.
31. "Open to the Public—Season '80" (May, 1980), 70.

Chapter 10

1. For detailed notes respecting individual pieces in the Collection and, where known, their makers and/or provenance, see inventories in each room at Woodford Mansion prepared by June Avery Snyder, 1980 edition. Pictorial and descriptive material respecting a very early state of the Collection appears in M. Rodman Street, "A Dutch Colonial House at Paoli," *Philadelphia Suburban Life* (Oct. 1909): 1; respecting the Collection as it was in 1931 and 1932, in Joseph Downs, "An Eighteenth Century Philadelphia Mansion," *The Antiquarian* (New York, May, 1931), frontispiece, 26, and "Woodford—A Colonial House of 1734–1756," *Good Housekeeping* (Oct., 1932), 54; and in the years 1947–1959, in John P. B. Sinkler, *The Naomi Wood Collection Woodford Mansion* (1947 and later printings).
2. Wallace Nutting (Boston, 1921), 80, illus. p. 77.
3. (Phila., 1976, Lib. Cong. no. 76-3170), 157, item 124a. See also references there cited.
4. Wallace Nutting, *The Furniture Treasury* (Framingham, Mass., 1928), 2: fig. 2669.

Chapter 11

1. George B. Tatum, *Philadelphia Georgian* (Middletown, Conn., 1976), 38, 62.
2. *Ibid.,* 64; Earle, *History of Fairmount Park,* 94; "Old Fairmount Park Mansion Being Restored," *Philadelphia Inquirer,* Dec. 2, 1928.
3. Robert C. Smith, "Two Centuries of Philadelphia Architecture," in *Historic Philadelphia,* ed. Luther D. Eisenhart (Phila., 1953), 289, 291.

4. Fiske Kimball, *Domestic Architecture of the American Colonies* (New York, 1922), 88, 89.
5. See Samuel Wetherill, Jr., Woodford insurance survey, 9th mo. 5th, 1769, Philadelphia Contributionship.
6. A narrowing of the hall to the rear is apparently explained in Wise and Beidleman, *Colonial Architecture for Those About to Build*, 45.
7. Henry J. Kauffman, *The American Fireplace* (Nashville, 1972), frontispiece, 106.
8. Peterson, *The Carpenters' Company 1786 Rulebook*, pl. 27, also illustrated in Tatum, 105.
9. Smith, "Philadelphia Architecture," 291–292; Kauffman, *American Fireplace*, 68.
10. Tatum, *Philadelphia Georgian*, 77–78.
11. Lillian I. Rhoades, *The Story of Philadelphia* (New York, 1900), 357; Francis B. Brandt and Henry V. Gummere, *Byways and Boulevards in and about Historic Philadelphia* (Phila., 1925), 70; Samuel, *A Word Sketch of Fairmount Park* (Phila., 1926), 13; Earle, *History of Fairmount Park*, 94. And see Marie Kimball, "The Revival of the Colonial," *Architectural Record* (July, 1927), 1, 5.
12. Eberlein and Lippincott, *Colonial Homes of Philadelphia*, 133; Cousins and Riley, *Colonial Architecture of Philadelphia*, 20.
13. Tatum, 76.
14. Inventory of the Estate of William Coleman, Estate no. 235 of 1769.
15. HSP MS Collns, item AM .9108.
16. Charles E. Peterson, report "Old Buildings at Woodford," Sep. 29, 1971, and "Preliminary Notes on the Evolution of Woodford," July 28, 1975, Naomi Wood Trust records.
17. *Pa. Gazette*, May 6, 1756.
18. Katherine D. Neustadt, *Carpenters' Hall: Meeting Place of History* (Phila., 1981), 6–8.
19. Wainwright, *Colonial Grandeur in Philadelphia*, 8.
20. *Idem*; Tatum, 50, 52; Charles E. Peterson, "Robert Smith, 1722–1777," typescript, Jan. 2, 1981, Carpenter's Company of Philadelphia.
21. Directors' Minutes, Phila. Contributionship, Sep. 5, 1769.
22. Gunning Bedford, survey Nov. 3, 1772, Philadelphia Contributionship.
23. Fiske Kimball, *Domestic Architecture*, 110.
24. William R. Ware, *The Georgian Period* (Boston, 1900), pt. 6: pls. 4, 5.
25. See photograph, Smith, "Philadelphia Architecture," 292, fig. 7, and comment, 293. For exterior and interior photos of the structure, see Philip B. Wallace, *Colonial Houses, Philadelphia Pre-Revolutionary Period* (New York, 1931), 90–102; for interior photos, Harold D. Eberlein and Cortlandt V. Hubbard, *Colonial Interiors, Third Series* (New York, 1938), pls. "Woodford"; and for measured drawings, American Institute of Architects, *Old Philadelphia Survey Drawings* (1931–1932), at Free Library of Philadelphia. See also Joseph P. Sims, "Architectural Checklist of Historic Buildings in the Philadelphia Area," *PMHB* 68 (1944): 194.
26. Kauffman, *American Fireplace*, frontispiece.
27. Marie Kimball "Revival of the Colonial," 6.
28. Fiske Kimball, *Domestic Architecture*, 101.
29. See H. C. Metz plan, "Topography 1870 Vicinity of Woodford Mansion," at Fairmount Park Commission (appears to have been prepared from plan ca. Oct., 1870 by Theodore Cuyler, Park engineer).
30. Charles E. Peterson, "The Tenant House," in *Preliminary Report on improvements planned for Woodford Mansion Complex*, Aug. 20, 1975, for Fairmount Park Commission.
31. Fairmount Park Commission, file "Woodford."
32. Metz plan, note 29 above.
33. "Topographical Map of Fairmount Park," *Third* and *Fourth Annual Reports of the Commissioners* (1971 and 1972), frontispiece.
34. See Eberlein and Hubbard, *Colonial Interiors, Third Series*, pls. "Woodford," for restoration paint colors.
35. *Report of Chief Engineer for 1925*, 3.
36. For an enthusiastic description of Woodford in that year, see James D. Van Trump, "Pavilion on the Schuylkill," *Charette Magazine* (Pittsburgh Architectural Club, May 1962), 15.